EXPLORING THE
BLACK HILLS
& BADLANDS

D0062792

EXPLORING THE
BLACK HILLS & BADLANDS

HIRAM ROGERS

A Cordillera Press Guidebook
Johnson Books: Boulder

Library of Congress Cataloging-in-Publication Data
  Rogers, Hiram.
    Exploring the Black Hills and Badlands: a guide for hikers, cross-country skiers, and mountain bikers / Hiram Rogers.
        p.   cm.
    Includes bibliographical references and index.
    ISBN: 1-55566-111-4
    1. Outdoor recreation—Black Hills Region (S.D. and Wyoming)—Guidebooks. 2. Outdoor recreation—North Dakota—Badlands Region—Guidebooks. 3. Black Hills Region (S.D. and Wyoming)—Guidebooks. 4. Badlands Region (N.D.)—Guidebooks.   I.Title.
GV191.42.B53R64   1993
796.5'09783'9—dc20   93-24675
                                                                    CIP

Front Cover Photograph:
Sage Creek Wilderness *Badlands National Park*
Back Cover Photographs:
Mountain Biker, Little Spearfish *Tim Schoon*
Limestone and Fawns *Edward Raventon*
Cover Design: Bob Schram/Bookends

First Edition
1 2 3 4 5 6 7 8 9

Printed in the United States of America by
Johnson Printing Company
1880 South 57th Court
Boulder, Colorado 80301

WARNING: Hiking, skiiing, or biking in mountainous terrain can be a high-risk activity. This guidebook is not a substitute for your experience and common sense. The users of this guidebook assume full responsibility for their own safety. Weather, terrain conditions, and individual abilities must be considered before undertaking any of the hikes in this guide.

CONTENTS

ACKNOWLEDGMENTS

This guide would not have been possible without the help of many people. Mike Besso and Walt Borneman nurtured the manuscript through its formative stages. Galen Roesler and Marty Dumpis of the Black Hills National Forest kindly reviewed substantial portions of the manuscript. Joe Zarki, Badlands National Park; Karri Fischer and Gary Kiramidjian, Wind Cave National Park; John Corey, Craig Pugsley, and Sally Svenson, Custer State Park; Dale Houstman and Dave Brandt, Custer Ranger District; Scott Spleiss, Harney Ranger District; Betsey Greene and Rod Brown, Pactola Ranger District; Paul Bosworth, Spearfish Ranger District; Brian Daunt, Elk Mountain Ranger District; Jerry Hagen, Bearlodge Ranger District; Tony Gullett and Marty DeWitt, Bear Butte State Park; Dennis Boucher, Fort Meade Recreation Area; Kim Raap, South Dakota Department of Game, Fish, and Parks; Jane Gyhra, Devils Tower National Monument; Bruce Kaye, Theodore Roosevelt National Park; and John Tunge, Little Missouri State Park, all reviewed manuscripts concerning their areas of responsibility. Dick Fort, Everett Follette, and Jim Hunter also reviewed trail descriptions.

On my own trips in the Black Hills and Badlands I've enjoyed the company of various hikers, mountain bikers, and skiers. Craig and Stacey Hall, Bob Nutsch, Eric and Laura Caddey, Tod Leferve, Karl and Nitro Marlowe, Kathy, Leroy and Sophie Hart, Doug and Morgan Thompson, Don Gifford, Brad Young, Sandy Snyder, and Mike Besso have all patiently endured long trips filled with mapping and photography stops. Without their companionship and enthusiasm this guide would never have been finished, nor would any of the trips have been as fun.

BLACK HILLS AND VICINITY

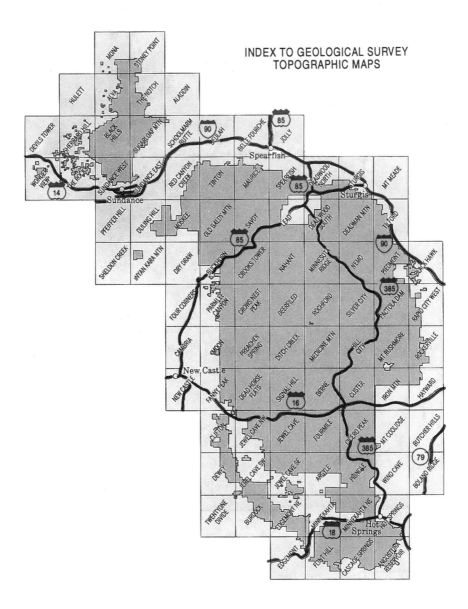

INDEX TO GEOLOGICAL SURVEY
TOPOGRAPHIC MAPS

INTRODUCTION

This guide describes hiking, cross-country skiing, and mountain biking trips in the Black Hills and Badlands region. Many of the routes are also open to horses. The Black Hills area includes Black Hills National Forest, Wind Cave National Park, Custer State Park, Bear Butte State Park, and Devils Tower National Monument. To the north and east of the Black Hills are some of North America's best examples of Badlands topography, well represented by Badlands National Park, Theodore Roosevelt National Park, and Little Missouri State Park. South Dakota's Centennial Trail is the only long trail in the region and is described in its entirety.

The Black Hills and Badlands form a distinct geographic subunit of the northern Great Plains. Both regions are characterized by extremes of weather and by a lack of water. The limit of Pleistocene glaciers helps to define the boundaries of this guide. The Black Hills were never glaciated, while the higher ranges to the west in the Rocky Mountains were heavily glaciated. The Missouri River in the Dakotas roughly marks the limit of continental glaciation. The water-rich terrain left behind by the glaciers east of the Missouri River is much different from the dry prairie west of the river.

This is not a comprehensive guidebook. While nearly every trail in the region was hiked and considered for the guide, only the "best" trips are included. Some allowances were made to provide a variety of geography, ecology, and levels of difficulty. If your favorite trip was left out, I apologize.

The trips described here range from short, self-guided interpretive trails, such as Rankin Ridge in Wind Cave National Park, to multiday expeditions, such as the Sage Creek Wilderness in Badlands National Park. While every trip may not be suitable for everyone, there are trips for families with children and trips for experienced backpackers looking for off-trail excitement. There are trips for hikers, skiers, mountain bikers, and equestrians.

Winter is the season to explore the cross-country ski trails in the northern Black Hills. Cool temperatures, without lingering snow, make spring travel ideal in the southern Black Hills or in the Badlands. In summer, escape from the heat of the prairie lowlands to higher areas in the Black Hills such as the Norbeck Trails around Harney Peak. In fall, dry soil and mild weather combine to make superb hiking and mountain bike riding anywhere in the region.

Each trip begins with a brief description. The general location refers to a straight line distance from the nearest town. Detailed information on how to reach each trailhead is provided. Distances are given for each trip, and often for optional variations. You'll also find out which maps you may need, and whom to contact for more information. Please note that most of the trails described here are newer than the current U.S. Geological Survey quadrangles, and thus are not shown on the maps. Many of the trails are also not shown on the current Black Hills National Forest map.

In most cases, trail distances were measured with an odometer on a mountain bike. Measured distances are listed as tenths of a mile. Less reliable distances and distances measured solely from maps are given in fractions of a mile.

The detail of each route description corresponds to the difficulty of finding the route. Descriptions for well-marked trails are brief, while descriptions of obscure trails are very detailed. Descriptions for some sections of the Centennial Trail are lengthy due to both the distance covered and the number of potential trouble spots.

Road networks in the Black Hills National Forest are constantly evolving. In the Black Hills, and to a lesser extent in the Badlands, there are many more roads than are shown on U.S. Geological Survey or Black Hills National Forest maps. Avoid the temptation to navigate solely by watching road intersections. I have simplified the Black Hills National Forest road classification system by calling all roads by number. These roads are generally permanent, are signed, and have numbers such as BHNF Road 607-1D. The degree of upkeep and signing varies greatly between district offices. Roads lacking numbers or signs should not be considered permanent.

Trail systems throughout the Black Hills and Badlands are being expanded and improved. Major relocations are planned for the Centennial Trail in the Nemo Ranger District in the northern Black Hills and for the Norbeck trail system. New trails are under construction at Theodore Roosevelt National Park, the Sundance Trails in the Bearlodge Mountains, and Spearfish Ranger District. Be aware that a trail guide cannot remain current forever, and that the conditions of trail markers can deteriorate over time. It's a good idea to check your map each time you stop on an unfamiliar trail or route and to check with the appropriate management agency before starting on an unfamiliar trail. In addition to the maps in this guide, you should always carry a Black Hills National Forest map when travelling in the Black Hills.

Day trips in the Black Hills and Badlands require only a little advance planning. You need to know the length of the route, and remember to check if the trip requires a car shuttle. In summer your main worries are sun and wind protection. Handy items to carry include food, water, first aid kit, sunscreen, lip balm, and a hat for shade. Few trailheads provide drinking water and you should never drink untreated water in the Black Hills or Badlands. Snakes, bison, and other wildlife can pose hazards for hikers. Do not disturb any wildlife you encounter. Poison ivy grows in many moist areas.

Mountain bikers should also prepare for their trips. Special equipment includes tools, tire pump, patch kit, and money to call for a ride if things go wrong. Riders should wear a helmet and gloves for those inevitable crashes.

Preparation for cross country skiers should include dressing in layers and drinking plenty of water since dehydration can reduce your resistance to the cold. Wind protection is essential and it is always a good idea to carry extra gloves and a hat.

Skiers will learn to adapt to the pattern of Black Hills winters. Often snowfalls are followed by rapid warming, so it is important to try to ski soon after a storm, before the snow melts. Even during the harshest cold spells, midday temperatures may moderate enough for pleasant outings. By late winter, midday temperatures often climb well above freezing. This creates wet, soft snow that can stick to ski bottoms like glue. To avoid this "snowball snow" start your trip early and avoid the midday melt.

By late spring the repeated freeze and thaw of the snowpack builds a hard, thick crust on the surface of the snowpack. Ideally, skiers can glide on, and often skate across, this crust without breaking through. Unfortunately, this hardpack only forms over small areas and seldom lasts long.

Backpacking in the Black Hills differs little from that in other areas. Badlands backpacking, on the other hand, can be quite different. The major difference is that some areas have no water and you must pack all of yours in. The weight and bulk of a large water supply can be a major burden on a long trip, so many parties elect to hike in a short distance and set up a base camp. The intricacies of the Badlands landscape make competent map and compass use a necessity. Getting lost in Sage Creek is a real possibility. Careful attention to your map in any Badlands area will allow you to plan a more efficient and enjoyable route.

RIDE, STRIDE, OR GLIDE
HINTS FOR MULTIPLE USE

Most outdoorspeople own hiking boots, skis, and a mountain bike, and use them all as the seasons change. Many trails and routes in the Black Hills National Forest are open to all three uses, and deciding how best to travel on a particular route may be a challenge. Unless otherwise noted, trails in National Park Service units are closed to mountain bikes. All National Park Service units in this guide very rarely receive enough snow for skiing.

Only a few hiking trails in the Black Hills National Forest are too rough for mountain bikes. Crow Peak and the Centennial Trail in Elk Creek, and around Samelius Peak, are probably the most difficult. You may be able to ride these trails, but for mere mortals, walking is easier and more enjoyable. Cross-country hikes are not suited for mountain bikes. Bikes are not allowed on the Flume Trail or in the Black Elk Wilderness. Mountain bikers should also note that it is illegal to ride trails in the national parks, Devils Tower, or in Custer State Park north of U.S. 16A, except the Centennial Trail.

To help mountain bikers in selecting their trips, the footway for each trip is described as either a single-track trail, two-track dirt road, maintained dirt road, or gravel road. Skiers and mountain bikers should note that terrain that is exciting on a bike is often equally exciting on skis. All the cross-country ski areas in the northern Black Hills are fun to ride in summer. The easiest mountain bike rides in this guide are the two on the Black Hills Burlington Northern Heritage Trail. Intermediate rides include Custer Peak and Holey Rock.

Hikers can, of course, do any trip in this guide. A few trips, such as Burno Gulch, Ward Draw, and Bear Mountain use gravel roads, and only parts of such routes will be of interest to hikers. Hikers should note that all of the cross-country ski trails established by the Black Hills National Forest follow abandoned roads. The best easy hikes include Rankin Ridge and the Door or Notch trails. Good intermediate hikes include Crow Peak, Harney Peak–Sylvan Lake, and Caprock–Coulee. The most rugged off-trail trips in the Black Hills National Forest—Sylvan Peak, Spearfish Peak, French Creek, and Sand Creek—can only be done on foot. The longest hikes included are Sage Creek, Centennial Trail, Norbeck East, and Achenbach.

Skiing in the Black Hills is limited in most winters to a poorly defined snowbelt which includes the Limestone Plateau and the northern Black

Hills around Lead. Bear Mountain is the southern limit, and there is rarely skiable snow south or east of Galena. The snowbelt is criss-crossed by the Black Hills snowmobile trail system, so get a copy of the snowmobile trails map and check it before trying out any new routes. Use this map to learn where not to go. Many routes that look good in the summer will be covered with snowmobile tracks come winter. You should also note that in some winters the "snowbelt" does not extend beyond the range of the snowmaking equipment at the downhill ski area on Terry Peak.

Beginning cross-country skiers should try the Black Hills Burlington Northern Heritage Trail, Lead, or A Loop at Big Hill. Long ski loops such as Bear Mountain, Swede Gulch, or Ward Draw should be attempted only by strong, experienced groups.

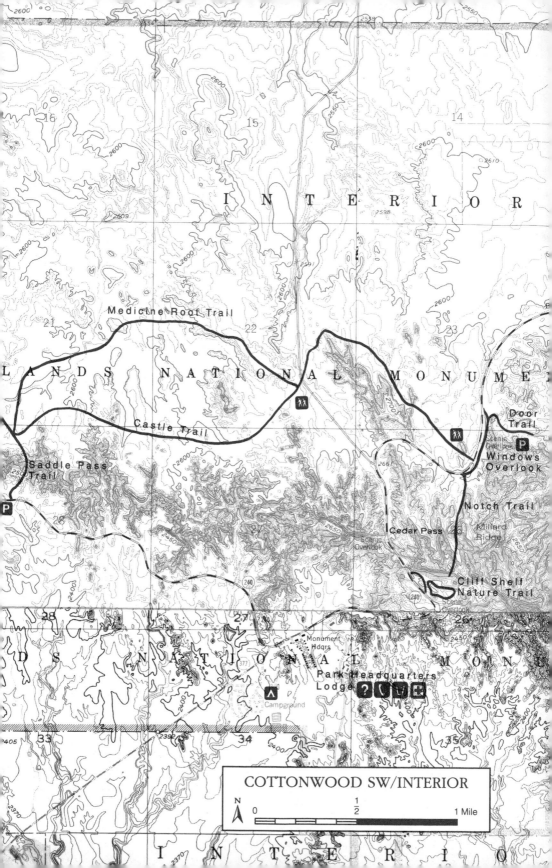

COTTONWOOD SW/INTERIOR

BADLANDS NATIONAL PARK

Door, Notch, and Window Trails
BADLANDS NATIONAL PARK

▲ **Description:** Three short, easy trails that leave from the Windows parking area.

▲ **General Location:** Five miles northeast of Interior, South Dakota.

▲ **Access:** From Interior, drive 2 miles northeast on South Dakota 377 to the park loop road. Turn right onto the loop road and drive about 2½ miles to the Windows parking area. The parking area can also be reached by taking Exit 131 from Interstate 90 and driving south past the Badlands National Park Northeast Entrance Station.

▲ **Distance:** The Door Trail is a ¾ mile round trip, the Notch Trail is a 1½ mile round trip, and the Windows Trail is very short.

▲ **Maps:** Badlands National Park Hiking Trails; USGS 1:50,000 Badlands National Park Special Topographic Map.

Most of the trails in Badlands National Park are located on the east side, just north of the Ben Reifel Visitor Center. Four trails leave from the Windows parking area. The Castle Trail leads west, while the Door, Window, and Notch trails explore the Badlands to the east. These three trails can be combined for a leisurely half day of hiking.

The Window Trail is just a short walk from the parking area to an overlook. The Badlands below form the head of the Rake Creek drainage. Millard Ridge forms the west and south sides of the upper basin.

The Notch Trail leaves from the south end of the parking area. The trail wanders south in a small draw before climbing steeply on a ladder. The trail ends at a dramatic "window" in the Badlands Wall that overlooks the Cliff Shelf Nature Trail.

The Door Trail leaves from the north end of the parking area. This is an interpretive trail that focuses on the geologic history of the park. Stops along the trail illustrate the formation of the ash beds, fossil soils, and claystones that are exposed along the route. The role of water in depositing, cementing, coloring, and finally sculpting these rocks is also explained.

The rocks exposed higher on Millard Ridge are part of the Oligocene Sharps formation. The Sharps is mostly pinkish tan siltstone, but the lowest layer, called the Rockyford Member, is a thick ash bed. Below the Sharps is the Oligocene Brule formation. Brule formation rocks form most of the Badlands Wall and contain abundant oreodont (a camel-like mammal) and turtle fossils. Brule formation rocks are diverse and include clay, silt, sand, volcanic ash, and fossil soil beds.

Badlands National Park has two other interpretive trails. The Fossil Exhibit Nature Trail concentrates on paleontology, while the Cliff Shelf Nature Trail explores the ecology of a slump block area. Slump blocks are the few areas in the Badlands that are able to hold moisture for plants.

All of these trails are well marked and easy to follow. Hikers in any Badlands should protect themselves from heat, wind, and sun. Use these trails to familiarize yourself with the Badlands landscape, then try the Castle Trail or visit the Sage Creek Wilderness on your next hike.

For More Information: Contact Badlands National Park, P.O. Box 6, Interior, SD 57750, (605) 433-5361 or 433-5362.

Medicine Root–Castle Trails Loop
BADLANDS NATIONAL PARK

▲ **Description:** An easy day hike along the northern edge of the Badlands Wall.

▲ **General Location:** Two miles west of the Badlands National Park Ben Reifel Visitor Center near Interior, South Dakota.

▲ **Access:** Drive 2 miles west of the visitor center on the park loop road to the Saddle Pass Trailhead. The trailhead can also be reached by driving 28 miles east from Wall, South Dakota, on South Dakota 240 and the park loop road.

▲ **Distance:** About a 5-mile loop.

▲ **Maps:** Badlands National Park Hiking Trails; USGS 1:50,000 Badlands National Park Special Topographic Map.

Hiking in Badlands National Park is a much different experience than hiking in the Black Hills. Besides the obvious differences in topography and elevation, the contrast between lush prairie and stark, barren Badlands makes hiking in the park unique. The Medicine Root Loop and the

Saddle Pass and Castle trails can be combined into a loop hike which serves as an excellent introduction to hiking in the park.

The Saddle Pass Trail is a short, steep climb, but provides a relatively easy route from the base of the Badlands Wall to the grasslands above. One-half mile from the parking area the trail ends at an intersection with the Medicine Root loop and Castle Trail. Follow the Castle Trail for two miles to the east as it skirts the top of the wall. Along the way the trail passes through the sod tables, massive pinnacles, and steeply eroded gullies characteristic of the Badlands.

Just before the Castle Trail reaches the gravel Old Northeast Road, turn left at a poorly marked intersection onto the Medicine Root Trail. The loop swings north away from the wall into the grasslands. Follow the loop back to the junction with the Saddle Pass Trail and descend Saddle Pass to return to the trailhead.

Badlands National Park contains world class deposits of fossils from the Oligocene Epoch, but the Medicine Root loop is not recommended for fossil hunters. Few fossils are found along the route and it is illegal to disturb any fossils in the park without a permit.

In addition to its famous fossil heritage, the park is known for bizarre Badlands landforms. The combination of soft, easily eroded sediments, dry climate, and sudden torrential rains produce extremely high rates of erosion. The most prominent feature in the park is the Badlands Wall, which is an erosional boundary between lower grasslands in the plain of the White River and an upper plain of grasslands. The wall is a succession of pinnacles and vertical knife-edge ridges carved into the soft sedimentary rocks. The wall is composed of poorly consolidated clay and ash beds. Steep canyons and gullies cut the wall intermittently, providing access between the two levels of grasslands. Learning to follow gullies and ridge systems over the crumbling sediment and being able to climb the wall are essential skills for exploring off trail in the most rugged parts of the park.

The grasslands support a variety of wildlife. Deer, antelope, coyotes, and bighorn sheep are found within the park. The park also supports a small herd of bison which are commonly found in the many prairie dog towns. Magpies and meadowlarks are the most common birds. Hikers in the grasslands grow accustomed to the constant soft chirping of the ever-present meadowlarks. Cliff swallows and grouse are also found.

Buffalograss, western wheatgrass, needle and thread grass, and blue grama are the most common prairie grasses in the park. Few trees can grow in the arid climate. Hardy junipers are restricted to small slump blocks where the broken sediments can hold enough shallow groundwater.

Hikers should prepare differently for a hike in the Badlands than for a hike in the Black Hills. Heat, lack of water, and absence of shade are the most important factors. Warning: This hike can be hot. This hike can be very hot. Carry water. Carry lots of water. Hot sun and persistent dry winds can cause dehydration and severe sunburn. Use sunscreen liberally and wear a hat for protection from the blazing sun.

For More Information: Contact Badlands National Park, P.O. Box 6, Interior, SD 57750, (605) 433-5361 or 433-5362.

Sage Creek Area, Badlands Wilderness
BADLANDS NATIONAL PARK

▲ **Description:** Off-trail hiking through the heart of the Badlands Wilderness.
▲ **General Location:** Eight miles south of Wall, South Dakota.
▲ **Access:** From Interstate 90 in Wall, drive 8 miles south on South Dakota 240 to the junction with the Sage Creek Rim Road, which leads west. There is easy access at the Sage Creek Campground, but it is possible to enter the Badlands Wilderness from almost anywhere along this road. The Conata Picnic Area is a convenient starting point for trips on the east side of the wilderness.
▲ **Distance:** There are no marked trails.
▲ **Maps:** USGS Badlands National Park 1:50,000 Special Topographic Map.

The 64,250 acres preserved in the Badlands Wilderness make it easily the largest wilderness in the northern Great Plains. The heart of the wilderness is the west side of the north unit of Badlands National Park, commonly known as Sage Creek. This is a land of profound solitude and quiet. It is also a place that will change your idea of what wilderness really is. To most Americans, wilderness is rugged, alpine mountains too steep and too rocky to have been altered by man. Sage Creek meets none of these expectations, yet is far wilder than most alpine ranges.

There are no maintained trails in the Sage Creek Wilderness. A trail is shown on the topographic map leading south in a loop from the Sage Creek Campground, but it is unmaintained and indistinguishable from the hundreds of buffalo trails that cross the Badlands. Based on my experience, I can recommend no particular route over any other, but must rely on the advice of a friend who said, "Just tell them to go there, they'll have fun."

The north boundary of the wilderness is roughly defined by the Badlands Wall, which divides the upper grasslands from lower grasslands in the White River watershed. The "baddest" badlands in the park lie along the wall and in a basin south of Pinnacles Overlook. To reach the roughest places you will need to climb the wall. The wall is not high, but the steep, crumbling slopes can be dangerous. A rule of the thumb is to not climb anything you would not want to slide down. Sage Creek and McGinty passes cross the Wall, and there is another easy pass in Section 25 between Hay Butte and Deer Haven.

If you enjoy scrambling on the Wall, you will definitely enjoy the rest of Sage Creek Wilderness. Perhaps the best way to explore is to follow a drainage as far to its head as you can. Often the draws are so steep, and the meanders in them so tight, that you must walk almost sideways to follow the channel that the runoff has carved. The more resistant rock layers form shelves that can be used to connect adjacent drainages. Throughout the wilderness the hiker sees a constantly changing array of the towers, pinnacles, and tables characteristic of the Badlands.

Fossils are easy to find on the east side of Sage Creek Wilderness. Remember that it is illegal to disturb any fossils that you may find. Westward in Sage Creek elevation increases and the rocks become older. Most of the bedrock around the main forks of Sage Creek is sandstone and clay of the Eocene Chadron formation. To the east, the flat areas are covered with the eroded remains of Chadron and Brule formation rocks. The wall itself is composed of Brule formation, and landslide deposits shed from it.

Deer Haven is the most prominent landslide in the wilderness. Landslides break up the impermeable clay and ash-rich sediments. Water from subsequent rainfalls can be trapped in the broken sediments. Juniper trees tap the groundwater and their roots help to stabilize the wildly jumbled surface. Deer and other animals use the juniper groves for shelter, the landslides have then created small oases in the Badlands.

Wildlife watching is spectacular in the wilderness. Bring binoculars and a telephoto lens for your camera. Buffalo can often be found grazing in the main forks of Sage Creek. Give these giants plenty of space, since there is nowhere for you to hide if they become annoyed. The park supports a small herd of bighorn sheep which may be found near the Pinnacles or Deer Haven. The wilderness also contains several prairie dog towns. Conata Basin, inside Badlands National Park, is being considered as an reintroduction site for the endangered black-footed ferret. Ferrets feed on prairie dogs and were decimated by prairie dog eradication programs.

If you must have a goal for your hike, there are three obvious trips to try. Deer Haven is easy to reach from Conata Picnic Area, or you can try to follow the Old Loop Trail south of the Sage Creek Campground. A longer trip circles Hay Butte via Sage Creek Pass. However, it is easier to go wherever the terrain leads you. Once in rugged Badlands it can be difficult to pinpoint your location, and it is possible to spend all day exploring a very small area.

To fully appreciate Sage Creek Wilderness you should camp overnight. For as long as you stay there will be no interruption from the modern world. You will probably not see another person, and may not see a footprint but your own. There are almost none of the relics of mining or ranching that you might see in other wildernesses. The remains of a few homesteads can be found, but the Badlands are too wild and too formidable to have been settled for long.

No permits are necessary to camp overnight in the backcountry of Badlands National Park. Be prepared to be baked and dried by the sun, and buffeted and dehydrated by the wind. At all costs avoid the Badlands after one of the rare heavy rains as the water turns the clay and ash into an impenetrable sea of gumbo. This is a stark landscape subject to extremes of temperatures. For milder conditions, it is best to visit in the spring or fall.

For More Information: Contact Badlands National Park, P.O. Box 6, Interior, SD 57750, (605) 433-5361 or 433-5362.

SOUTH DAKOTA CENTENNIAL TRAIL

Norbeck Dam to NPS Road 5
WIND CAVE NATIONAL PARK

▲ **Description:** A scenic hike along the south end of the Centennial Trail through mixed prairie and forest.

▲ **General Location:** Ten miles north of Hot Springs, South Dakota.

▲ **Access:** The Norbeck Dam Trailhead is the southern terminus of the Centennial Trail. A small parking area on the east side of South Dakota 87 is located 0.6 mile north of the junction of South Dakota 87 and U.S. 385 and is 0.3 mile north of the start of the Lookout Point Trail (WCNP Trail 4). The trailhead can also be reached by driving south 6.4 miles on South Dakota 87 from the boundary of Wind Cave National Park and Custer State Park. The Highland Creek Trailhead is located 1.4 miles east of South Dakota 87 on NPS Road 5.

▲ **Distance:** This section is 6 miles one way.

▲ **Maps:** Black Hills National Forest Map; Centennial Trail User's Guide; USGS Wind Cave and Mt. Coolidge, South Dakota, 7.5-minute quadrangles.

The Centennial Trail begins in mixed prairie and woodland along the southern flank of the Black Hills in Wind Cave National Park. The meeting of forest and prairie provides excellent opportunities to view bison, elk, deer, and other wildlife where they utilize both habitats for forage and shelter.

From the trailhead at Norbeck Dam, drop north into the valley of Beaver Creek and then meander downstream to the east. The route follows an old grassy road past Reaves Gulch and Curley Canyon before turning north at the head of a large meadow, where the trail leaves the Beaver Creek valley at two miles. Long-distance hikers now have a tough job ahead, for this is the low point on the Centennial Trail until it leaves the Black Hills near the Black Hills National Cemetery.

WIND CAVE QUADRANGLE

Ascend from Beaver Creek, first steeply and then steadily. Reach an open area and turn right onto a faint old road which leads north. Follow this road to a junction with an old fire road at 4.5 miles, which may be signed as WCNP Trail 5. Stay on the Centennial Trail and follow the old fire road northeast, crossing two small gullies. After passing the pens used for holding bison during the park's annual fall roundup, you reach the Highland Creek Trailhead on NPS Road 5 at 6 miles.

The National Park Service calls the Centennial Trail "Trail 6" in Wind Cave National Park. Much of the route follows faint, overgrown jeep trails. Trails are marked with carsonite posts and blazes, and trail intersections are marked with bison-proof posts. Throughout its length, the Centennial Trail is marked by brown carsonite (similar to fiberglass) posts with the number 89 and the symbol of the appropriate managing agency. In some places mileage posts are placed along the trail, but both types of trail markers are used as scratching posts by bison and can be easily flattened.

Travelling across open prairie is hot, dry work in the summer. Hikers unfamiliar with this terrain should be careful not to underestimate the full effects of powerful sun and limited shade. Mountain bikes are not allowed on any of the hiking trails in the park, but bikers can ride on the park's gravel roads.

For More Information: Contact Wind Cave National Park, Route 1 Box 190, Hot Springs, SD 57747, (605) 745-4600.

NPS Road 5 to French Creek Horse Camp
CUSTER STATE PARK

▲ **Description:** A trip through the south half of Custer State Park for hikers, mountain bikers, and equestrians.
▲ **General Location:** Eleven miles southeast of Custer, South Dakota.
▲ **Access:** The Highland Creek Trailhead is 1.4 miles east of South Dakota 87 on NPS Road 5. To reach the French Creek Trailhead drive 2.6 miles east of South Dakota 87 on Custer State Park Road 4. The Blue Bell lodge, general store, and campground are located at the junction of CSP Road 4 and South Dakota 87.
▲ **Distance:** This section is 9.5 miles one way.
▲ **Maps:** Black Hills National Forest; Centennial Trail User's Guide; Custer State Park Trail Guide; USGS Mt. Coolidge, South Dakota, 7.5-minute quadrangle.

The Custer State Park section of the Centennial Trail leads from mixed prairie and woodlands into terrain more typical of the eastern Black Hills. The land is heavily forested and deeply dissected by meandering streams. The topography is rolling with numerous small ridges

and divides. Since the Black Hills were not covered by ice during the Pleistocene glaciation, streams draining off the uplifted core of the hills have been free to cut their own channels, rather than being confined to straight, U-shaped valleys left by glaciers. French Creek Gorge is a wonderful example of the valleys cut by these streams, and is similar to the terrain along the Centennial Trail through Boxelder Forks Canyon near Nemo in the northern Black Hills.

From the Highland Creek Trailhead, enter Custer State Park by crossing through a gate in the bison fence. The route follows an old road along a broad, open ridge. Pass a faint trail to the west that may be signed "Coe Pocket" and continue northwest along an unnamed drainage. Near Coe Pocket is a line of foundations and overgrown furrows which are all that remain from an old farm that was located nearby. Cross another gate through a bison fence which runs along the Section 6/31 boundary. This southern part of Custer State Park is excellent for seeing bison; just be sure to give these giants a wide berth. The Centennial Trail is now a faint path as it crosses a small divide into the Flynn Creek drainage and then follows an old, faint road along the south fork. Cross two dry forks of Flynn Creek and hike gradually upstream along the southwest side of the bed of the main fork. Turn west away from Flynn Creek, then follow a small gully north to reach gravel CSP Road 7 at 3.5 miles.

Cross CSP Road 7 and continue north as the route follows an old road to ascend a small ridge. Then turn east down a small draw. The trail next turns north to skirt the west edge of a meadow. After passing another small draw, enter another meadow regaining sight of the Wildlife Loop Road. Beyond this meadow, pass by one gully and turn up the second, still following a faint road. The trail then skirts the edge of a larger meadow before turning sharply east down a prominent draw to reach the Wildlife Loop Road (CSP Road 1) at 7.5 miles.

To stay on the Centennial Trail, cross the Wildlife Loop Road and follow an old dirt road up a small draw before exiting east and climbing a small divide. Continue on this road northeast into the broad, open valley of French Creek, reaching CSP Road 4 at 9 miles. Blue Bell Lodge and Resort are located 2.1 miles west at the junction of CSP Road 4 and South Dakota 87. Continue east on CSP Road 4 to reach the French Creek Horse Camp Trailhead at 9.5 miles.

Prospectors with Lieutenant Colonel George Armstrong Custer's 1874 Black Hills expedition first found gold in the Black Hills along French Creek, confirming decades of rumors. Their discovery triggered one of the largest and wildest gold rushes in the history of the West, culminating in the discovery of the rich Deadwood placers in the northern Black

Mt Coolidge

Lookout Tower 6023

BM 5539

36

CT Bypass Trail

Galena

BM 4813

5497

French Creek Route

BM 4560

French Creek Primitive CG

BM 4602

Blue Bell

French Creek Horse Camp

TH

Creek

CSP #4

BM 4698

Wildlife Loop

MT. COOLIDGE QUADRANGLE

N

0   ½   1 Mile

Hills. However, geologists with Custer's party were skeptical about the French Creek discovery. There has been speculation that one of the goals of Custer's expedition was to find gold. There has been only minor placer gold mining along French Creek, and today the area is the major natural area in Custer State Park. Perhaps the doubts of the geologists were well founded.

The Custer State Park section of the Centennial Trail is open to mountain bikes and horses. Custer State Park marks the Centennial Trail with plenty of blazes and carsonite posts. No drinking water is found along the trail, the French Creek Horse Camp has the first water available to northbound hikers. Supplies can be purchased at Blue Bell Lodge and Resort.

For More Information: Contact Custer State Park, HC 83 Box 70, Custer, SD 57730, (605) 255-4515 or 255-4464 for the Peter Norbeck Visitor Center in summer.

French Creek Horse Camp to Iron Creek Horse Camp
CUSTER STATE PARK

▲ **Description:** A trip through northern Custer State Park for hikers, mountain bikers, and equestrians.
▲ **General Location:** Five miles east of Custer, South Dakota.
▲ **Access:** To reach the French Creek Trailhead drive 2.6 miles east of South Dakota 87 on Custer State Park Road 4. The Blue Bell lodge, general store, and campground are located at the junction of CSP Road 4 and South Dakota 87. From the intersection of U.S. 16A and South Dakota 87 in Custer State Park drive 1.6 miles east on U.S. 16A to CSP Road 9. Drive 0.9 mile south on CSP Road 9 to the Badger Hole Trailhead. To reach Iron Creek Horse Camp take South Dakota 87 to gravel Black Hills National Forest Road 345, which is the Camp Remington Road. Turn left onto BHNF Road 345.2A and drive about one-half mile to the trailhead.
▲ **Distance:** This section is 11.5 miles long one way.
▲ **Maps:** Black Hills National Forest; Centennial Trail User's Guide; Custer State Park Trail Guide; USGS Mt. Coolidge and Iron Mountain, South Dakota, 7.5-minute quadrangles.

The northern part of Custer State Park is wilder and has fewer roads than the southern part. The Centennial Trail here offers more solitude, though the forest setting offers fewer vistas. Mountain bikers especially will enjoy the rolling section of trail north of Legion Lake.

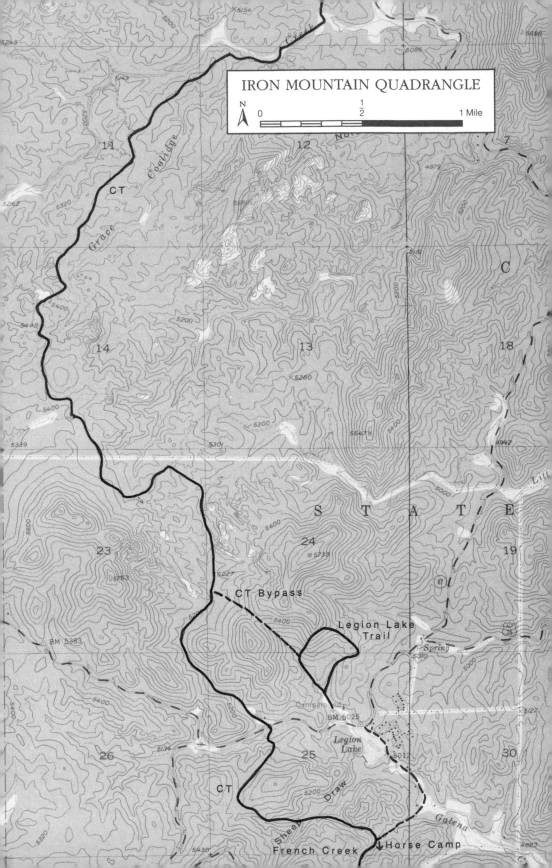

From the French Creek Horse Camp Trailhead cross a gate onto a dirt road. Follow this dirt road beside French Creek, passing a cabin and a side road to the west. Leave the road to follow a tributary of French Creek to the north. From this point the road continues east along French Creek, and leads to a campsite in the French Creek Natural Area.

The Centennial Trail, meanwhile, makes up for the gentle grade of the last mile and a half by climbing steadily out of the valley of French Creek. The climb may in fact be too steep for horses or mountain bikes. Soon the south end of a bypass trail is reached at 1.5 miles. The bypass trail follows an old road to the northeast, while the main trail ascends three switchbacks to reach a new high point at 5,437 feet.

From the ridge, descend to the southern limit of the 1988 Galena fire. South Dakota's version of the 1988 Yellowstone fires was also the result of extended drought, but was not caused by long term build-up of forest fuels. This lightening-caused fire burned 1,700 acres. Custer State Park uses both selective logging and controlled burns to manage its forests. Like the Yellowstone fires, the Galena fire totally devastated some areas, but regrowth has also been rapid.

The Centennial Trail crosses several roads and fire lines built during the fire which may obscure the trail before reaching the north end of the bypass trail which follows an old dirt road uphill at 2.75 miles. The trail then climbs over a small ridge crossed by a powerline. At the bottom of the next descent, another bypass trail for horses and bikes leads east and then northwest to the Legion Lake Lodge and Campground. The Centennial Trail follows an old dirt road over a divide into Sheep Draw, then mercilessly over another divide and back down to Galena Creek and U.S. 16A at 4.75 miles.

From U.S. 16A the Centennial Trail follows a prominent tributary of Galena Creek northwest through the last of the prime bison viewing terrain. In Custer State Park, the main trail rejoins the bypass trail from Legion Lake in an open draw. The route continues along an old dirt road past a ridge lined with spectacular pinnacles. Then climb to a junction with a dirt road near a powerline and follow this road, crossing under the powerline to another road junction. The roller coaster descent from this point to the Needles Highway may offer the best section of mountain biking along the entire Centennial Trail. Keep an eye peeled for euphoria-crazed bikers as the trail winds past a junction with a side road leading east. Then drop alongside Grace Coolidge Creek and climb a ridge northwest of the creek. President Calvin Coolidge and his wife established their summer White House in Custer State Park in 1927. Many of the park's features, including Mount Coolidge, the highest point in the main body of Custer State Park, still visible to the south, were named for the Coolidges. Pass several old roads left from logging operations, then reach a sign explaining the park's Big Squaw logging unit. The open, park-like appearance of this area is a typical result of logging operations in the park.

At the north end of the ridge, drop east again beside Grace Coolidge Creek and follow it to a grassy ridge where the trail turns north into a side drainage. The trail then climbs over a small divide, to descend again to the Needles Highway (South Dakota 87) at 10.75 miles, just east of a junction with BHNF Road 345 to Camp Remington.

To continue north on the Centennial Trail cross the Needles Highway. The trail crosses the boundary between Custer State Park and the Black Hills National Forest before reaching BHNF Road 345.2A and the Iron Creek Horse Camp Trailhead at 11.5 miles.

Water, supplies, and camping are available at Legion Lake. No other drinking water is found along the route.

Between French Creek Horse Camp and U.S. 16A, there are two bypass routes for horses and mountain bikers. The bypass trail north of French Creek is 2.5 miles long, and the bypass trail by Legion Lake is 1.8 miles long. Designed to bypass sections of steep, newly built trail, these routes will doubtless be considered challenges by some parties. Groups on short trips can use the bypass trails to form short loops and avoid retracing their route.

For More Information: Contact Custer State Park, HC 83 Box 70, Custer, SD 57730, (605) 255-4515 or 255-4464 for the Peter Norbeck Visitor Center in summer.

Iron Creek Horse Camp
to Big Pine Trailhead
BLACK HILLS NATIONAL FOREST

- ▲ **Description:** A moderate hike through the Norbeck Wildlife Preserve and Black Elk Wilderness.
- ▲ **General Location:** Five miles southwest of Keystone, South Dakota.
- ▲ **Access:** To reach Iron Creek Horse Camp take South Dakota 87 to gravel BHNF Road 345 which is the Camp Remington Road. Turn left onto BHNF Road 345.2A and drive about one-half mile to the trailhead. Big Pine Trailhead is located on the north side of South Dakota 244, 2.9 miles west of Mount Rushmore.
- ▲ **Distance:** This hike is 8.2 miles long.
- ▲ **Maps:** Sierra Club Hiking Map of the Norbeck Wildlife Preserve; Black Hills National Forest Norbeck Wildlife Preserve and Black Elk Wilderness; Centennial Trail User's Guide; USGS Mount Rushmore and Iron Mountain, South Dakota, 7.5-minute quadrangles.

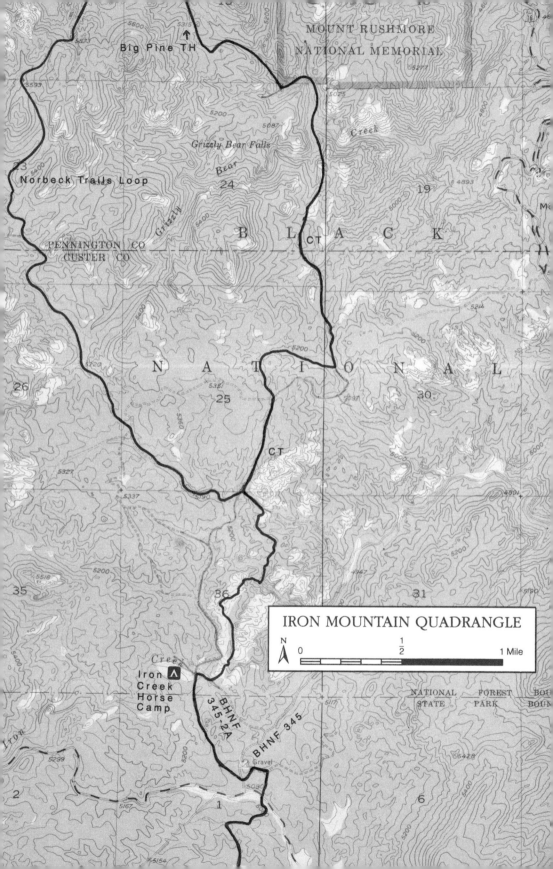

MOUNT RUSHMORE
NATIONAL MEMORIAL

Big Pine TH

Grizzly Bear Falls

Norbeck Trails Loop

Creek

Grizzly Bear

B L A C K
CT

PENNINGTON CO
CUSTER CO

N A T I O N A L

25

CT

Iron
Creek
Horse
Camp

Creek

BHNF 345-2A

BHNF 345

Gravel

Iron

NATIONAL   FOREST   BOU
STATE   PARK   BOUN

IRON MOUNTAIN QUADRANGLE

N   0   1/2   1 Mile

This section of the Centennial Trail crosses the only designated wilderness in the Black Hills. Wilderness designation prohibits the use of motorized vehicles and mountain bikes, although the Black Hills National Forest is currently developing a Centennial Trail bypass for mountain bikes around the wilderness. The Centennial Trail crosses the little-travelled east side of the Norbeck trail system through an area of profound solitude and true wilderness experience.

From the trailhead at Iron Creek Horse Camp, hike north on a trail constructed in 1992. Climb over a small ridge, then cross Iron Creek on a bridge. Hike along the west side of a group of spires, then climb to a ridge with views to the west of Harney Peak. Descend to cross an intermittent creek. Climb up and over one more granite ridge to reach a junction with Trail 15 at 1.3 miles.

Turn left and follow Trail 15 northwest on BHNF Road 346 for 0.2 mile to an intersection with Trails 3 and 7. At the junction are a rugged group of spires from which Harney Peak can be seen. Follow the Centennial Trail and Trail 3 north up a dry side draw to a four-way junction at 2 miles. BHNF Road 347 leads west from the junction and Trail 16 leads east. Follow the Centennial Trail and Trail 3 north, immediately passing an old gravel pit.

Descend to reach a small draw and old logging road leading east at 2.5 miles. Go up and over a small divide to reach another old logging road leading east at 2.6 miles. Pass one more side road east before reaching the Black Elk Wilderness boundary in a small draw at 3.1 miles.

Once in the wilderness, hike north to Grizzly Bear Creek, then up a side draw to a junction with Trail 5 at 4.1 miles. The Centennial Trail follows Trail 5 across a small corner of Mount Rushmore National Memorial and reaches a junction with abandoned Trail 10 at 4.6 miles. Continue north on Trail 5 to pass over the divide between Grizzly Bear and Pine creeks. Cross through a spectacular line of spires just before reaching the junction with Trail 14 at 5.8 miles.

Continue to follow Trail 5 west to a branch of Pine Creek. Follow the branch north to the main stem, then head upstream to another small draw. Follow the draw north to a divide which forms the Black Elk Wilderness boundary at 7.3 miles. Descend Trail 5, which is now an old road, to a trail junction at 7.6 miles.

Turn right onto the Centennial Trail where Trail 5 continues west. Hike northeast, crossing a network of old logging roads to reach South Dakota 244 at 8.2 miles. The Big Pine Trailhead is across the highway.

The Black Hills National Forest plans to develop a bypass trail around the Black Elk Wilderness for use by mountain bikes. In conjunction with development of the bypass trail, names and numbers of the trails

MOUNT RUSHMORE QUADRANGLE

in the Norbeck Wildlife Preserve will be changed, although no more trail relocations are planned.

If you're hiking the entire Centennial Trail, but want to climb Harney Peak, try an alternate route along Trails 7, 9, and 5. Though longer, this route includes a beautiful hike along Grizzly Creek as well as the top of Harney Peak.

For More Information: Contact Custer Ranger District, 330 Mount Rushmore Road, Custer, SD 57730, (605) 673-4853.

Big Pine Trailhead to Dakota Point Trailhead
BLACK HILLS NATIONAL FOREST

▲ **Description:** A rugged hike from South Dakota 244 to Sheridan Lake.
▲ **General Location:** Seven miles northwest of Keystone, South Dakota.
▲ **Access:** The Big Pine Trailhead is on the north side of South Dakota 244, 2.9 miles west of Mount Rushmore. To reach the Samelias Trailhead drive 3 miles west on U.S. 16 from the junction of U.S. 16 and 16A, or drive 2.6 miles east on U.S. 16 from the 16/385 junction. The trailhead is on the north side of the road. To reach the Flume Trailhead, drive 1.7 miles north on U.S. 385 from the junction with U.S. 16. Turn east on paved BHNF Road 192 for 0.7 mile. Then turn left onto a paved road toward the South Marina and reach the Flume or Calumet Trailhead at 1.5 miles. The Dakota Point Trailhead is located 1.6 miles east of U.S. 185 on the Sheridan Lake Road (Pennington County C228) and 0.3 mile south on dirt BHNF Road 434.
▲ **Distance:** 13 miles one way.
▲ **Maps:** Black Hills National Forest; Centennial Trail User's Guide; USGS Mt. Rushmore, South Dakota, 7.5-minute quadrangle.

One of the roughest sections of the Centennial Trail lies between the northern limit of the Harney Peak trail system and Sheridan Lake. Unsuspecting mountain bikers accustomed to relatively easy riding elsewhere on the Centennial Trail are easily lured onto this section, then mangled by steep grades, tight turns, and a boulder-strewn trail. Determined bikers can make it through this section, but it is much easier to walk.

Hikers will have the opposite experience, and enjoy the trail because of the solitude it offers. The roughest section, between Samelias Peak and BHNF Road 392 at Sheridan Lake, is a rough single track, but no more difficult to hike than any other well-travelled, but poorly maintained hiking trail in the Rocky Mountains.

MOUNT RUSHMORE QUADRANGLE

Hike north from the Big Pine Trailhead, ignoring three forks that lead right, to reach a single track at 0.1 mile. Descend to reach paved BHNF Road 353 in the valley of Battle Creek at 0.5 mile. Cross the road and a set of railroad tracks, then follow dirt BHNF Road 354-1E along a small draw which leads northeast. Crest a small divide and turn right, then left at a junction at 1.6 miles. The left turn leads onto a single track through a narrow draw.

At 1.9 miles the Centennial Trail enters a meadow, then follows a series of old dirt roads leading northwest. At 3 miles turn onto a single track and then cross under U.S. 16 in a highway underpass. Head east above the highway embankment to reach the Samelias Trailhead at 3.5 miles.

From the Samelias Trailhead, switch back up to a prominent saddle on the west side of Samelias Peak. At 4.1 miles turn right onto dirt BHNF Road 531. Follow Road 531 past a junction with Road 531-1A and over a small saddle. Then turn onto an overgrown logging road at 5 miles. This is the point where the difficult mountain biking begins. The road quickly becomes a trail which contours east, then north. At 6.1 miles reach another saddle and begin the climb up Mount Warner. At 6.8 miles the summit of Mount Warner is just a short bushwhack to the west. From the top of the 5,889-foot high summit, Harney Peak looms over Elkhorn Ridge. Mount Rushmore, Samelias Peak, and Hill City are also visible.

Beyond Mount Warner, the Centennial Trail follows a rough ridge to the north. At 7.8 miles turn east off of the ridge to briefly follow a grassy logging road. The trail turns north, then east, and follows a rugged set of ridges over boulders of Precambrian Age quartzite. Descend the ridges to reach BHNF Road 392 at 10 miles.

North of BHNF Road 392 the trail becomes much easier to ride on a mountain bike. Traverse a ridge north to reach the Flume (or Calumet) Trailhead on the shore of Sheridan Lake at 10.7 miles. The Centennial Trail follows the Flume Trail for the next mile along the bed of the historic flume. At 11.7 miles leave the Flume Trail. Just beyond, a bypass trail for horses leaves to the right to go around Sheridan Dam.

The Centennial Trail crosses the dam and ascends a stairway made of slabs of slate. The trail crosses Spring Creek on a large bridge. At 12.7 miles the horse bypass trail reenters the main trail from the right. The trail then follows BHNF Road 381 west to reach a locked gate and the Dakota Point Trailhead at 13 miles.

The town of Sheridan was founded in 1875, soon after A. J. Williams discovered gold along Spring Creek. The town was initially named Golden City, a name which proved too optimistic. Placer mining in

Spring Creek was short lived and none of the hardrock mines around Sheridan proved productive. The town was briefly deserted in 1876 when its miners joined the stampede to Deadwood, but recovered to become the first seat of Pennington County. The town then dwindled to a few small ranches that were covered when the waters of Spring Creek became impounded behind Sheridan Dam.

With the exception of a short section between Dakota Point and Sheridan Dam, the Centennial Trail here is well marked by blazes, carsonite posts, and the occasional Silver Arrow. This entire section is closed to motorized vehicles, although few signs indicate this closure.

For More Information: Contact Harney Ranger District, HCR 87, Box 51, Hill City, SD 57745, (605) 574-2534; or Pactola Ranger District, 803 Soo San Dr., Rapid City, SD 57702, (605) 343-1567.

Dakota Point Trailhead
to Deer Creek Trailhead
BLACK HILLS NATIONAL FOREST

▲ **Description:** A long hike or mountain bike ride from Sheridan Lake to Pactola Reservoir.
▲ **General Location:** Ten miles northeast of Hill City, South Dakota.
▲ **Access:** The Dakota Point Trailhead is located 1.6 miles east of U.S. 385 on the Sheridan Lake Road (Pennington County C228) and 0.3 mile south on dirt BHNF Road 434. To reach the Brush Creek Trailhead drive 8.6 miles north of U.S. 16 on U.S. 385. Turn east and drive 2.9 miles on BHNF Road 159. Turn left onto BHNF Road 772 and drive 0.3 mile to the trailhead. To reach the Rapid Creek and Tamarack trailheads, drive 2 miles south past South Dakota 44 on U.S. 385 to Pactola Dam. Switch back for 0.5 mile down a gravel road to an offset four-way junction. From the junction, the Rapid Creek Trailhead is 0.1 mile to the left and the Tamarack Trailhead is 0.7 mile straight ahead on the main gravel road. To reach the Deer Creek Trailhead drive 1.4 miles north of South Dakota 44 on U.S. 385 to the paved Silver City Road (Pennington County 321). Drive 0.3 mile west on the Silver City Road, then 0.1 mile west on a dirt road.
▲ **Distance:** 16.3 miles one way.
▲ **Maps:** Black Hills National Forest; Centennial Trail User's Guide; USGS Silver City, Pactola Dam, and Mt. Rushmore, South Dakota, 7.5-minute quadrangles.

If any section of the Centennial Trail is ideal for a mountain bike ride, it is the section from Dakota Point to Deer Creek. Close access to U.S. 385 makes it easy to shuttle cars and ease the burden of this long haul.

While the entire section is hilly, none of the hills are long or difficult. If you feel up to the challenge of a long trip on the Centennial Trail, this is the section to try.

From the Dakota Point Trailhead, go west for 0.2 mile to a powerline, then turn north onto a trail. At 0.7 mile, cross the Sheridan Lake Road and continue north. Go right at the next fork, which leaves the main draw, then turn left onto a dirt road at 1.4 miles. At 2 miles cross unmarked BHNF Road 551 and then turn left in an aspen grove onto another dirt road.

At 2.6 miles turn left at a junction in a small saddle, then left again onto a dirt road. Watch carefully as the trail gradually diverges from the road. The trail crosses a gate and passes two cattle-fouled springs on the next descent. BHNF Road 160 is crossed at a three-way junction at 3.5 miles.

At the triple junction take the northwest fork and follow it for 0.1 mile before turning off onto a trail that leads into the Bald Hills. The Bald Hills are heavily grazed, and following the Centennial Trail through an assortment of trails and old roads requires a sharp eye. Exit the Bald Hills at 4.8 miles on a ridgetop which offers a view west of the Seth Bullock Fire Tower on Scruton Mountain.

Follow the ridge to the east, drop off the north side, cross a gate and then reach a fork of Victoria Creek at 5.6 miles. Cross another gate near the divide with Brush Creek. Then cross BHNF Road 159 before reaching the Brush Creek Trailhead and BHNF Road 772 at 6.4 miles.

Follow Road 772 northeast before turning north into Gold Standard Gulch at 7.2 miles. The next 0.7 mile in the tight, winding canyon is easily the prettiest part of this trail section. Exit the canyon at 7.9 miles and continue up the main stem of Gold Standard Gulch following and crisscrossing a dirt road. At 9.6 miles leave Gold Standard Gulch.

Climb to a saddle on the divide between Gold Standard and Tamarack Creek at 9.8 miles. A side trail from here leads west to an overlook above Pactola Reservoir. The descent from the divide is confused by many intersections with old roads, but the Centennial Trail eventually follows the main stem of Tamarack Creek to reach the Tamarack Trailhead at 10.9 miles.

From Tamarack Creek, the Centennial Trail winds through a wide plain below Pactola Dam to reach the Rapid Creek Trailhead at 11.5 miles. From the trailhead, cross Rapid Creek, then turn right off the gravel road onto a dirt road at 11.7 miles. Pass a side road to the east, then turn right, then left at road junctions to reach a ridge crest at 12.3 miles. The trail climbs over one more ridge before crossing U.S. 385 at 12.8 miles.

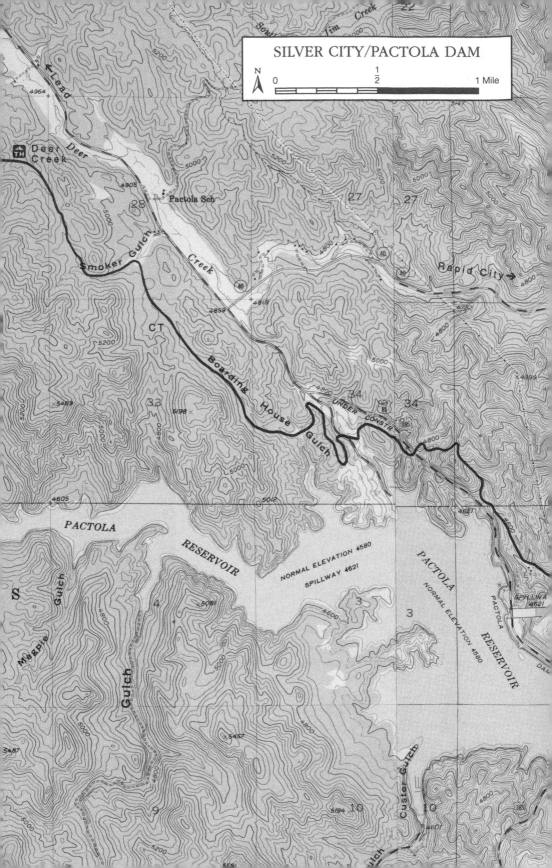

SILVER CITY/PACTOLA DAM

N
0   1/2   1 Mile

South Tim Creek

Lead

Deer Creek

Deer

Pactola Sch

Smoker Gulch

Creek

CT

Boarding House Gulch

UNDER CONSTR

Rapid City →

PACTOLA

RESERVOIR

NORMAL ELEVATION 4580

SPILLWAY 4621

PACTOLA

NORMAL ELEVATION 4580

PACTOLA

RESERVOIR

SPILLWAY 4621

PACTOLA DAM

Magpie Gulch

Gulch

S

Custer Gulch

The Centennial Trail crosses paved BHNF Road 264 at 13.3 miles. At 13.5 miles the trail reaches a ridgetop on the east side of Boardinghouse Gulch and a rusted sign indicating that an overlook above Pactola Reservoir is one-quarter mile south. Follow the ridgetop for one-half mile to a four-way junction and go straight through the junction on a two-track dirt road. The trail follows this road for a mile then is a single track briefly before descending to the bottom of Smoker Gulch, and its scenic trailer park, at 15.3 miles.

Beyond Smoker Gulch, follow dirt roads north to 16.2 miles where the trail drops on switchbacks to the paved Silver City Road. Just past the road a short side trail leads right to the Deer Creek Trailhead at 16.3 miles.

The Centennial Trail from Dakota Point to Deer Creek traverses a sea of ponderosa pine and slate. Deer, which adapt easily to an environment altered by man, are the most common wild animals. Cattle graze along many parts of this section.

The name Pactola is derived from Pactolus, the mythical Lydian river of golden sands. The name reflects the lofty, but unfulfilled, hopes of the miners who prospected Rapid Creek during the 1875 gold rush.

It should be obvious from the route description that route finding on this section of the Centennial Trail is made difficult by many intersections with two-track dirt roads. But the route is not as complicated as it may sound, and most travellers should be able to follow the blazes and carsonite posts. Most of this section also follows the route of the old Silver Arrow Trail and many of those old markers are still in place.

Although the Centennial Trail is, in theory, closed to motorized vehicles from Dakota Point to Deer Creek, only one small sign indicates this closure. Consequently, use by vehicles on the road segments and ATV's on the trail is substantial. The Pactola Ranger District plans to install "No Motorized Vehicle" signs on the trail in 1993.

For More Information: Contact Pactola Ranger District, 803 Soo San Dr., Rapid City, SD 57702, (605) 343-1567.

Deer Creek Trailhead to Boxelder Forks Campground
BLACK HILLS NATIONAL FOREST

▲ **Description:** A moderate hike or mountain bike ride through the Central Black Hills.
▲ **General Location:** Between the towns of Silver City and Nemo, South Dakota.

NEMO/SILVER CITY

N

0      $\frac{1}{2}$ 1 Mile

▲ **Access:** For the Deer Creek Trailhead drive 23 miles south of Pluma, or 1.4 miles north of South Dakota 44, on U.S. 385 to the Silver City Road (Pennington County 321). Drive 0.3 mile west, then 0.1 mile on a dirt road to the trailhead. The Pilot Knob Trailhead is 2.9 miles farther north on U.S. 385 and 1 mile east on BHNF Road 208. Boxelder Forks Campground is located 2.1 miles west of Nemo on BHNF Road 140. It is possible to shuttle cars via the Nemo Road and BHNF Road 208.
▲ **Distance:** This hike is 10.2 miles long one way.
▲ **Maps:** Black Hills National Forest; Centennial Trail User's Guide; USGS Nemo and Silver City, South Dakota, 7.5-minute quadrangles.

The central Black Hills have a look and feel all their own. This is an area dominated more by pine and slate than any other in the hills. Dense coats of ponderosa pine have crowded out almost all other vegetation. Even along streams there are few woody shrubs or grasses. The bedrock is slate, broken only sporadically by quartz. Slate weathers to form thin, nutrient-poor soils further reducing diversity in vegetation. Still, the area has rugged topography suitable for challenging trips.

From the Deer Creek Trailhead follow a single track north for 0.6 mile before turning left onto a dirt road. Stay right at the next two forks. After 1.3 miles turn right onto a well-travelled dirt road behind a house and a trailer. Follow this road to U.S. 385 at 1.9 miles, then turn right onto gravel BHNF Road 202. At 2.4 miles turn left onto a dirt road by a powerline, then climb over a small divide. After 3.3 miles cross BHNF Road 208 and reach the Pilot Knob Trailhead.

The Centennial Trail south of Pilot Knob is supposed to be closed to motor vehicles, but no signs indicate the closure, and there are no structures in place to prevent vehicles from using the trail.

From Pilot Knob the Centennial Trail follows a rough jeep road for 1.7 miles over a divide to reach unmarked BHNF Road 152 in the valley of the west fork of Estes Creek. At 5.6 miles leave Road 152 north on a trail which climbs over another small divide to reach BHNF Road 740 in the valley of the main fork of Estes Creek at 6.6 miles.

Follow Road 740 west and at 6.8 and 7.1 miles turn right onto progressively less-used side roads. At 7.4 miles reach an active timber sale. Climb over a saddle then turn left onto unmarked BHNF Road 152 by a beautiful cabin. At 8.5 miles reach a gravel road and turn right to pass through a gate. The 1.2 miles of trail beyond the gate are the highlight of this section as the trail passes through the spectacular upper canyon of Boxelder Creek. Fall is the best time to hike Boxelder Canyon as you are more likely to stay dry on the eight crossings of Boxelder Creek in low water.

At 9.7 miles reach the Boxelder Forks Trailhead. Follow gravel BHNF Road 140 to reach Boxelder Campground at 10.2 miles. Hopefully, you

NEMO/PIEDMONT QUADRANGLES

N   0   ½   1 Mile

arranged a car shuttle via the Nemo Road and BHNF Road 208, otherwise its time to see this route from the other side.

Many people think of the Centennial Trail as being the first long-distance hiking trail in the Black Hills. In fact, the Centennial Trail uses much of the route of an earlier hiking trail. From U.S. 16 to Boxelder Campground the Centennial Trail follows the route of the former Silver Arrow Trail. The Silver Arrow Trail was a 55-mile-long trail developed by Black Hills area Boy Scouts as a place where scouts could complete their required fifty-mile wilderness hikes.

The Silver Arrow Trail started at Sylvan Lake and climbed Harney Peak before descending to Horsethief Lake and joining the present route of the Centennial Trail. It mostly followed BHNF roads to Boxelder Creek. The water supplies and many of the campgrounds described by Fielder in her 1973 book have mostly been abandoned, but alert hikers will notice many of the silver arrow trail markers still in place. As the Centennial Trail is gradually removed from roads onto constructed trail, fewer of the arrows will remain on the route to remind hikers of their place in history.

The Nemo district of the BHNF intends to expand much of the Centennial Trail between Pilot Knob and Boxelder Campground. Extensive ATV loops will be installed west of the Centennial Trail and will extend north toward Crystal Mountain. ATV users and horse riders will bypass Boxelder Canyon from BHNF Road 152 to Blue Draw. A trail for persons with disabilities will bypass a shorter section of the canyon. The roadless section of Boxelder Canyon will be designated as a walk-in fishery.

Current Black Hills National Forest maps show existing bypass routes for horses and ATV's around Boxelder Canyon, but these routes are not marked, nor recommended for use, because of massive logging operations along the main and north forks of Estes Creek.

For More Information: Pactola Ranger District, 803 Soo San Dr., Rapid City, SD 57730, (605) 343-1567; or Nemo Ranger District, P.O. Box 407, Deadwood, SD 57732, (605) 578-2744.

Boxelder Forks Campground
to Dalton Lake Campground
BLACK HILLS NATIONAL FOREST

▲ **Description:** A moderately difficult trip between Boxelder Creek and Little Elk Creek.
▲ **General Location:** Near the town of Nemo, South Dakota.

▲ **Access:** From Nemo, drive west on gravel BHNF Road 140 for 2.1 miles to Boxelder Forks Campground. To reach Dalton Lake Campground, drive 0.5 mile north on the Nemo Road to paved BHNF Road 26. Drive 3.6 miles north to gravel BHNF Road 224. Turn right onto Road 224 and stay on the main road for 4.1 miles to Dalton Lake. The trailhead and sign are 0.1 mile beyond the campground.
▲ **Distance:** 8.5 miles one way.
▲ **Maps:** Black Hills National Forest; Centennial Trail User's Guide; USGS Nemo and Piedmont, South Dakota, 7.5-minute quadrangles.

The Centennial Trail between Boxelder Forks and Dalton Lake campgrounds is far more diverse and scenic than the trail sections to the south. This hike features steep canyons and choice overlooks which serve as the hiker's reward for the climbs out of the canyons. On this hike you will also leave the Precambrian schist and slate of the central Black Hills behind, and enter the Phanerozoic sedimentary rocks that rim the Black Hills.

From Boxelder Forks Campground cross gravel BHNF Road 140 and pass through a gate which marks the start of a new relocation around Boxelder Creek. Climb on a rough road which leads to the south rim of the canyon. Work your way generally east along the rim on old jeep roads and on some new trail. There are several nice overlooks along the rim. Descend from the rim to the bottom of Blue Draw and then turn east to reach BHNF Road 140 at 1.7 miles.

Head west on BHNF Road 140 for one-quarter mile before turning north onto BHNF Road 140-1B at the end of the relocation. Follow Road 140-1B over the crest of a small divide, then descend to a four-way junction with BHNF Road 678 at 2.9 miles. Continue straight through the intersection on BHNF Road 678-1A for one-half mile. Then turn onto a cattle path which leads to the intersection of the paved Nemo and Dalton Lake roads at 3.7 miles.

Cross the Nemo Road then hike alongside the paved Dalton Lake Road for one-quarter mile to a gate. Beyond the gate, climb steadily. The next 2.4 miles of the Centennial Trail are very difficult to ride on a mountain bike because of steep grades and loose rocks. Finish your climb at 4.8 miles on a rocky, heavily logged limestone ridge. Follow the ridge northwest, then north while enjoying the views down into the open valleys north of Nemo. Leave the ridge at a poorly marked switchback just short of a powerline. Descend two switchbacks to reach a dirt road at 6.4 miles.

Follow the smooth, two-track road east along contour and enjoy the many views down into Little Elk Creek Canyon. At 7.8 miles reach the start of another recent relocation. Continue on the dirt road east for

NEMO/PIEDMONT QUADRANGLES

N

0          $\frac{1}{2}$ 1 Mile

N

one-quarter mile, then descend a series of steep, rutted switchbacks on the west side of the Dalton Lake Ski Slide. At 8.5 miles reach BHNF Road 224 and the Dalton Lake Trailhead.

The Dalton Lake Ski Slide and Jump was built in 1935 by the Civilian Conservation Corps based in Nemo. This was the first ski area built in the Black Hills. One look down the steep, narrow runs is enough to convince anyone that downhill skiing in the 1930s was a more committing endeavor than it is today. Much of the ski slide is becoming overgrown, but it is still possible to imagine pioneer skiers on the slopes. The same crew also built the Dalton Lake Dam and Campground.

The first sale of timber from the U.S. Government was made to Homestake Mining Company in 1898. The Case One Timber Sale was located south of Nemo and just east of the Centennial Trail. The company bought all timber eight inches and more in diameter from a site on Estes Creek near Nemo. At that time, Homestake's mining operations in Lead used nearly five millon board feet and twenty thousand cords of wood in a single year, but logging on Case One still lasted until 1908. Homestake operated sawmills in Estes and Nemo until 1939. By 1988 two billion board feet of timber had been cut in the Black Hills National Forest, with half of that cut in the last twenty years.

There is no water along the trail from the crossing of Boxelder Creek at the mouth of Blue Draw to Dalton Lake Campground. Much of the trail is rocky and difficult to ride on mountain bikes. The trail will probably remain rocky as the Black Hills National Forest plans to keep this section of the Centennial Trail open to motorized vehicles.

The Nemo Ranger District plans a number of improvements to the Centennial Trail north of the Nemo Road. A new trail north of the Nemo Road will be built. The new trail will stay closer to the rim of Little Elk Creek Canyon and should be even more scenic than the current route. Near Waite Gulch a new side trail will extend east above Little Elk Canyon to an overlook above Red and White gates, two prominent narrow passages through the canyon. The last mile of this trail will be on land received by the Black Hills National Forest as part of a recent land exchange with Homestake Mining Company. The new Centennial Trail will then descend to Dalton Lake on the east side of the ski slide.

For More Information: Contact Nemo Ranger District, P.O. Box 407, Deadwood, SD 57732, (605) 578-2744.

Dalton Lake Campground to Point 5,045

BLACK HILLS NATIONAL FOREST

▲ **Description:** A moderate hike with one difficult section through Elk Creek Canyon.

▲ **General Location:** Ten miles south of Sturgis, South Dakota.

▲ **Access:** To reach Dalton Lake from Nemo, drive 0.5 mile north to paved BHNF Road 26. Follow paved Road 26 north for 3.6 miles to BHNF Road 224. Turn right on Road 224, and drive 4.1 miles, past the Dalton Lake Campground, to the trailhead. To reach the Elk Creek Trailhead from Sturgis, take Exit 32 off Interstate 90. Turn south and follow the signs for Wonderland Cave on BHNF Road 170. At 3.2 miles turn south onto gravel BHNF Road 135 for 2.8 miles. Then turn left onto dirt BHNF Road 168 and drive 2.4 miles to the trailhead. Elk Creek Trailhead can also be reached from I-90 on Exit 40. Turn south on the frontage road for 2.3 miles, then turn east onto unmarked BHNF Road 168. Drive 5.5 miles on Road 168 to reach a four-way junction before Bethlehem Cave. The trailhead is 1.5 miles farther on Road 168 which is signed "road closed in one mile." There is no access to point 5,045 at the north end.

▲ **Distance:** This section is 11.8 miles long one way. A 6.2-mile loop hike can be made by connecting the main Centennial Trail with the bypass around Elk Creek Canyon.

▲ **Maps:** Black Hills National Forest; Centennial Trail User's Guide; USGS Deadman Mountain, Piedmont, and Tilford, South Dakota, 7.5-minute quadrangles.

One of the most isolated sections of the Centennial Trail lies between Dalton Lake and the Black Hills National Cemetery. Within this isolation is Elk Creek Canyon, and perhaps the wildest and most rugged hiking in the Black Hills. A bypass trail for horses and mountain bikes has been built around the rougher eastern end of the canyon. Hikers can combine the bypass and main trails to form an exciting loop.

From the Dalton Lake Trailhead, cross Little Elk Creek and turn north onto the slope above the creek. The Centennial Trail follows a mix of dirt roads and trails until it reaches a spring and stock tank. Just beyond, at 1 mile, turn north onto gravel BHNF Road 704. At 1.5 miles, where Road 704 turns east out of the gulch, continue northwest on a dirt road. Another side road leads west at 1.9 miles, where the dirt road up the main fork is blocked by sandstone boulders.

Continue up the main draw keeping left at forks at 2.2 and 2.7 miles. At 2.8 miles pass another barricade, then turn left back onto BHNF Road 704 at 3.1 miles. The Centennial Trail climbs over a gentle saddle, crosses a gate and then turns north off Road 704 onto a trail at 3.4 miles.

DEADMAN MOUNTAIN/TILFORD

N

0       $\frac{1}{2}$ 1 Mile

The trail leads north along an open limestone ridge with views west into the headwaters of Elk Creek.

Descend steeply on switchbacks off the north side of the ridge. At the bottom of the descent, turn left onto a dirt road to reach a junction with BHNF Road 702 at point 4,486, at 4.1 miles. This is the south end of the bypass trail around Elk Creek Canyon. The main Centennial Trail leads east on Road 702 and crosses a gate before turning north onto a trail. Stay left at a fork, then descend steeply on switchbacks into Elk Creek Canyon.

Reach Elk Creek at 4.7 miles and turn west. For the next 1.5 miles the route winds through the deep canyon of Elk Creek. There is no pretense of a trail here, only a route along, across, and finally in the creek bed. High water every spring washes away any footway that develops. The canyon is choked with oak, ash, and willows. Steep limestone cliffs rise from the creek bed isolating the canyon floor. The bushwhack through the cobbles and boulders in the creek bed is very slow. Elk Creek is usually flowing at the east end, but is usually dry at the junction with the bypass at the west end.

At 6.2 miles, just beyond Bethlehem Cave, reach the junction with the north end of the Elk Creek Canyon bypass trail. The next 1.2 miles along the creek bed is easier as the trail follows an old railroad grade. At 7.4 miles turn north up a side draw. Follow a trail and old dirt road to reach the Elk Creek Trailhead and BHNF Road 168 at 8 miles.

From the Elk Creek Trailhead, follow a jeep road north for 0.1 mile, then turn left onto a trail. Climb over a small divide and follow old logging roads north to reach dirt BHNF Road 169 at 8.7 miles. At 8.9 miles turn north onto a grassy road and then left onto a trail along contour. The trail merges with a rough dirt road at 9.4 miles and continues generally north.

Leave the contour road by taking three consecutive right turns ending up at a sign for Road 613 (which is really BHNF Road 139) at 10.8 miles. Turn right onto the road and continue north to reach point 5,045 at 11.8 miles. There is no access to point 5,045.

To hike the bypass loop from the south end, continue west from point 4,486 on BHNF Road 702 and enter an active logging area. Go straight through a four-way intersection at a sign for the Big Elk Management Area. Pass a spring on the south side adjacent to a stone foundation and crumbling log cabin. Then pass side roads to the right, left, then right again in an area without trail markers. Pass one more side road leading south before reaching the Wonderland Cave Road (BHNF Road 137) at 1.5 miles. Paved BHNF Road 26 is 1 mile southwest on Road 137.

Cross BHNF Road 137 and follow a logging road along the crest of a ridge to the north. Descend the ridge through very heavy logging slash to reach a road along contour at 2.3 miles. Hike west along the road for about 100 feet and then follow a trail down switchbacks to the bottom of beautiful Dry Elk Gulch. Head east down Dry Elk Gulch, then climb steeply up the north side of the gulch. Gain the crest of the north ridge, then descend again to reach the main Centennial Trail in the bottom of Elk Creek Canyon at 4.1 miles.

Both the Centennial Trail and the bypass trail around Elk Creek are scheduled to be replaced by new trail construction in 1994. In addition to the new trail planned for Elk Creek Canyon, the entire route from Dalton Lake to the second crossing of BHNF Road 702 will be relocated off roads to a ridge to the west. A small relocation is also planned to take the trail off BHNF Road 137.

Anyone who has seen Elk Creek will find it difficult to imagine that a railroad once ran through the bottom of the canyon. But, Homestake Mining Company started construction in 1881 on a line down the canyon which reached Piedmont in 1890. The line was built to supply the underground gold mine in Lead with timber, but eventually added freight and passenger service. After frequent damage from fire and flood, the line was destroyed by a flood caused by heavy rain and melting snow in 1907. A few rough ties remain on the grade on the west end of the canyon, and one old rail remains near the mouth of Dry Elk Gulch.

A hike from Dalton Lake to point 5,045 illustrates the diversity of geology in the Black Hills. Downstream from Dalton Lake is a small outcrop of Archean Little Elk Granite. At 2.5 billion years old these are some of the oldest rocks in the Black Hills. To the north, around Elk Creek, the bedrock is Paleozoic sedimentary rocks, mostly massive beds of gently dipping Paha Sapa limestone. North of the Elk Creek Trailhead are Tertiary igneous quartz latite rocks of the Vanocker Laccolith, which are some of the youngest rocks in the Black Hills.

For More Information: Contact Nemo Ranger District, P.O. Box 407, Deadwood, SD 57732, (605) 578-2744.

Alkali Creek Trailhead to Point 5,045
BLACK HILLS NATIONAL FOREST

▲ **Description:** A difficult loop trip for hikers and mountain bikers.
▲ **General Location:** Five miles south of Sturgis, South Dakota.
▲ **Access:** From Interstate 90, take the Black Hills National Cemetery Exit 34.

Follow the frontage road on the east side of the interstate to a gravel road which leads into the Fort Meade Recreation Area. The Alkali Creek Trailhead is located 0.5 mile into Fort Meade on the east side of the road. There is no access to point 5,045.

▲ **Distance:** 13.6 miles round trip and 6.6 miles on the Centennial Trail one way.

▲ **Maps:** Black Hills National Forest; Centennial Trail User's Guide; USGS Tilford and Deadman Mountain, South Dakota, 7.5-minute quadrangles.

One of the most accessible sections of the Centennial Trail starts from the Alkali Creek Trailhead at Fort Meade. North from Alkali Creek, the trail leads over the Dakota Hogback to Bear Butte, while to the south it leads up Alkali Creek and Bulldog Gulch into the Black Hills. Hikers and mountain bikers seeking a long, rugged loop can combine the Centennial Trail south of the trailhead with BHNF Road 139.

Since most visitors will hike this section north to south, this trail description is given in that direction. From the Alkali Creek Trailhead, hike west along a slope which marks the point where Alkali Creek slices through the Dakota Hogback. Pass underneath Interstate 90 in a culvert (the south side is usually drier) 0.5 mile from the trailhead. Hike southwest on an overgrown two-track road to reach the Fort Meade/BHNF boundary at 1.1 miles.

The next 2.1 miles of trail into Bulldog Gulch were constructed in 1990 to avoid crossing private land that was on the old route at the mouth of Bulldog Gulch. The new trail was constructed as a foot trail and makes for difficult mountain biking because of the rough surface and steep grades. The trail follows Alkali Creek a short distance before ascending on switchbacks up a steep limestone dip slope. Eventually the trail reaches a southeast-trending ridge with good views of Bear Butte. Follow the ridge almost to the Fort Meade boundary, before dropping steeply into a tributary of Alkali Creek. After crossing the creek bottom, the Centennial Trail ascends steeply to a rocky, narrow sandstone ridge. The climb continues unrelentingly up switchbacks to reach another ridge which divides Alkali Creek from Bulldog Gulch, almost 1,000 feet above the trailhead. The descent from the ridge to BHNF Road 139 at 3.2 miles is also steep, but is a welcome relief from the climb from Alkali Creek.

Follow BHNF Road 139 east to the bottom of Bulldog Gulch at 3.7 miles, then turn southwest off the road onto a trail. For the next 0.9 mile the trail stays in the cobble-strewn bottom of the gulch. Mountain bikers wishing to bypass most of this section can follow a trail which leads south along contour from the point where the Centennial Trail first intersects Road 139.

DEADMAN MOUNTAIN/TILFORD

From the bottom of Bulldog Gulch, the trail climbs to a small divide and then reenters the main fork of Bulldog Gulch at 5.3 miles. The next 1.3 miles are steep, loose, and rocky as the Centennial Trail climbs on single track toward the headwaters of Bulldog Gulch. The trail intersects BHNF Road 139 on the ridge, which is the divide with Alkali Creek, at point 5,045 at 6.6 miles.

From this point, the Centennial Trail continues south to Elk Creek. Our loop however, turns north and follows BHNF Road 139 along the Alkali Creek–Bulldog Gulch divide for 3.8 miles back to the Centennial Trail in Bulldog Gulch. The first 1.1 miles of this road are rough and rocky, but the next 2.7 miles are smooth with rolling terrain that is perfect for mountain bikes. An added feature of the ridge-top route are the cool breezes which seldom penetrate into the gulches. Several overlooks along the ridge provide views southwest to the radio towers on top of Veterans Peak, the most prominent summit in this part of the Black Hills. After returning to the Centennial Trail–BHNF Road 139 junction in Bulldog Gulch, follow the Centennial Trail north for 3.2 miles back to the Alkali Creek Trailhead.

The Bulldog Gulch–Beaver Park area has been only lightly logged leaving a forest of ponderosa pine, aspen, and oak. The purple berries of Oregon grape are especially common in the understory. This corner of the Black Hills is steep and very rugged, off-trail hiking along the bottoms of the other gulches is difficult, but rewarding.

BHNF Road 139 forms the northwest boundary of the Beaver Park RARE II Area, and the proposed Beaver Park or Breakneck Wilderness. This is one of the six areas in the Black Hills recommended for wilderness designation by the Sierra Club and other conservation groups in 1992. Only Congress can designate a wilderness area, but the Black Hills National Forest is studying Beaver Park in order to decide whether or not to recommend wilderness designation to Congress.

This section of the Centennial Trail is well marked by blazes and carsonite posts. There is no drinking water found along the route, but water, toilets, and overnight camping facilities are available at Alkali Creek. For groups wishing to make an overnight trip on this loop, there is a small campsite at the bottom of Bulldog Gulch about 0.8 mile south beyond the junction with BHNF Road 139.

The Nemo Ranger District has proposed relocating much of the Centennial Trail from Pilot Knob to Alkali Creek. The goals of this project are to move the trail from roads onto trails constructed for hiking and to minimize conflicts between user groups. It is unlikely that the route for hikers will change north of BHNF Road 139, but much of the route to the south could be relocated. If Beaver Park is declared a wilderness area, mechanized vehicles, including mountain bikes, would be rerouted from upper Bulldog Gulch onto Road 139, which would then serve as a bypass trail.

For More Information: Contact Nemo Ranger District, P.O. Box 407, Deadwood, SD 57732, (605) 578-2744; or Area Manager, Bureau of Land Management, 310 Roundup, Belle Fourche, SD 57717, (605) 892-2526.

Alkali Creek Trailhead to Bear Butte Lake
FORT MEADE RECREATION AREA

▲ **Description:** A moderate hike, mountain bike, or horseback trip from the Dakota Hogback to Bear Butte Lake.
▲ **General Location:** One mile east of Sturgis, South Dakota.
▲ **Access:** For the Alkali Creek Trailhead, take Exit 34 from Interstate 90 to the frontage road east of the highway. Follow a gravel road 0.3 mile north into Fort Meade to the trailhead. The Fort Meade Trailhead is located one mile east of Sturgis, south of South Dakota 34, just inside the Fort Meade boundary. To reach the Bear Butte Lake Trailhead, drive 3 miles east of Sturgis on South Dakota 34, then 3 miles north on South Dakota 79. Turn left onto a gravel road which starts opposite the entrance to Bear Butte State Park. The trailhead is 0.2 mile down this road.
▲ **Distance:** 10.3 miles one way.
▲ **Maps:** Centennial Trail User's Guide; USGS Ft. Meade, South Dakota, 7.5-minute quadrangle.

The Fort Meade section of the Centennial Trail offers hikers, equestrians, and mountain bikers two distinct areas. To the south of South Dakota 34 the trail follows the high sandstone ridge known as the Dakota Hogback. In early spring this is some of the best mountain bike riding in the Black Hills. The sandy soil dries quickly and the area is too low to hold significant snowfall. This area can be ridden when much of the northern Black Hills are still snow covered or muddy. North of South Dakota 34 lies the only true prairie along the Centennial Trail. This section can be impassable when wet, but is usually clear by late spring.

From the Alkali Creek Trailhead, cross the gravel Fort Meade Road and head north through the prairie along the east side of the Dakota Hogback. After 0.4 mile turn west and climb steeply on a rough trail for 0.5 mile to the top of the Hogback Ridge. Catch your breath and then head north along the ridge top, enjoying views to the west of Bulldog Gulch and Beaver Park. Turn northeast off the ridge at 1.4 miles and descend on a rutted two-track jeep road to intersect the Fort Meade Road at 2.4 miles.

Cross the gravel road and follow a dirt two-track road, first northeast along the bottom of a small draw, then northwest up a steep hillside. The hilltop offers commanding views of Fort Meade and Bear Butte to the north. Cross a steep gulch just before reaching the Fort Meade Cemetery. Just beyond the cemetery at 3.9 miles, the Centennial Trail skirts the gravel road once more. Reach the Fort Meade Trailhead at 4.9 miles through an old barracks or stable area. Fort Meade was named in honor of Civil War hero General George G. Meade.

After leaving the Fort Meade Trailhead, the Centennial Trail crosses South Dakota 34 and 79, Bear Butte Creek, goes through a gate, and reaches the top of a gravel-covered hill at 5.9 miles. The trail follows the flat ridge top northeast and crosses another gate at 6.9 miles. Leave the ridge at a small saddle and follow a faint path north to a gate at 9.1 miles which marks the boundary between Fort Meade Recreation Area and Bear Butte State Park. The path is a portion of the historic Bismarck–Deadwood Trail. This trail section is marked only by carsonite posts which are easily knocked down by cattle. If you lose the trail, just continue generally towards the fence which marks the boundary and then head toward the gate.

Once into Bear Butte State Park, go east to the dirt (gumbo) access road at 9.3 miles. Follow the road a little further to 10 miles, then follow a trail east to the Bear Butte Lake Trailhead at 10.3 miles.

The old home of a major calvary outpost, Fort Meade now houses a veterans hospital. Also on the grounds is a museum dedicated to the story of the western calvary. The town of Sturgis was founded in 1878 in the shadow of the fort's protection and is named after Lieutenant Jack Sturgis, who died at the Little Bighorn under the command of Lieutenant Colonel George Armstrong Custer. The improved gravel road through Fort Meade is designated as a national backcountry byway. There is a self-guided tour brochure for the byway.

The ridge known as the Dakota Hogback circles the entire Black Hills and is separated from the hills by the Red Valley. Rapid erosion of the soft rocks of the Spearfish formation created the Red Valley. The hard sandstone of the Dakota formation resists erosion, consequently sandstone outcrops form ridges.

The section of the Centennial Trail located within the Fort Meade Recreation Area is administered by the Bureau of Land Management. The Alkali Creek Trailhead contains a six-unit, fee campground with water and toilets open from May 15 to September 30. The other trailheads have parking only. There is a campground on the north side of Bear Butte Lake within the state park. No drinking water is found along the trail.

Any trip on the Centennial Trail north of South Dakota 34 and 79 requires preparation for the sun and wind typical of the prairie. Mid-afternoon summer thunderstorms are common and trail users should remember that there is no shelter from these storms on the prairie.

For More Information: Contact Area Manager, Bureau of Land Management, 310 Roundup, Belle Fourche, SD 57717, (605) 892-2526.

Bear Butte Lake to Bear Butte Summit
BEAR BUTTE STATE PARK

▲ **Description:** A moderate hike to the north end of the Centennial Trail on top of Bear Butte.
▲ **General Location:** Nine miles northeast of Sturgis, South Dakota.
▲ **Access:** Drive 3 miles east of Sturgis on South Dakota 34, then 3 miles north on South Dakota 79 to the park entrance. The trailhead is located past the visitor center at the top of the loop road. From U.S. 79 turn left on the gravel road to Bear Butte Lake and drive 0.2 mile to the Bear Butte Lake Trailhead.
▲ **Distance:** 5.9 miles round trip from the Bear Butte Lake Trailhead or 3.1 miles round trip from the upper trailhead.
▲ **Maps:** Centennial Trail User's Guide; Bear Butte State Park Hiking Trail Guide; USGS Ft. Meade, South Dakota, 7.5-minute quadrangle.

Bear Butte is the most interesting of the short summit hikes in the Black Hills region and the climb to the top is one of the most popular hikes in the area.

From the Bear Butte Lake Trailhead head east 0.2 mile on the gravel road to South Dakota 79. Then follow the park road on the north side to 0.4 mile. Turn north, away from the road, and begin climbing an old two-track dirt road which parallels a fence. Cross a gate at 0.7 mile and reach another gate at 0.9 mile. The second gate is the north limit of horse travel on the Centennial Trail. From the gate, climb to the paved park road at 1.2 miles and follow the road to the Bear Butte Trailhead at 1.4 miles. This trailhead is the north limit for mountain bike travel on the Centennial Trail.

Most hikers will skip the preceding 1.4 miles and begin their climb of Bear Butte from the upper trailhead. The Centennial Trail follows the west side of the Ceremonial Trail to 2.15 miles, then the Summit Trail to 3 miles to finish at the top of Bear Butte. Observation platforms are located at the junction of the Ceremonial and Summit trails, at the top, and at an overlook 0.45 mile from the top. The climb is persistently steep and the summit a worthy end to the Centennial Trail.

Bear Butte is located outside of the Dakota Hogback that encircles the main part of the Black Hills, and thus offers a unique perspective. Deadman Mountain, Custer Peak, Terry Peak, and Spearfish Peak are the most prominent summits visible. At low light, a series of "circus rings" are apparent to the southwest. These rings are formed by the uplift of more resistant strata during the intrusion of the igneous rocks that formed Bear Butte.

The Ceremonial Trail forms a loop along the southern slopes of Bear Butte. Although the east loop is longer than the west loop, for variety, most hikers use the east loop to return to the parking area. The Ceremonial Trail was designated a national recreational trail by Congress in 1971 for its scenic, historic, and recreational opportunities. Bear Butte was registered as a national landmark in 1965 by the U.S. Department of the Interior.

A free self-guiding interpretive booklet for the Ceremonial Trail highlights the natural and cultural history of the area. The booklet is particularly helpful in the spring and summer when woody plants, wildflowers, and grasses are in bloom and easy to identify. The guidebook is scheduled to be replaced with trail signs.

The South Dakota Department of Game, Fish, and Parks maintains a visitor center below the trailhead. Displays focus on the geology of the mountain and the rich culture of the Plains Indian people for whom Bear Butte is a religious shrine. The park also maintains a small bison herd on the prairie below the visitor center.

Many Indian people continue to come to Bear Butte to participate in religious ceremonies. Prayer flags tied to trees are a common sight along the trails. Please do not disturb them. Also, to avoid conflicts with ceremonies, hiking off trail is prohibited in the park. Hikers are asked to avoid making unnecessary noise and to refrain from taking photographs or video taping individuals along the trail or near the camp area.

While trails in the park are short, the trails on Bear Butte are steep, rocky, and have numerous switchbacks. However, the trails are good for family groups with children. It is easy to gauge your progress while climbing, and the interpretive sites offer an excuse to stop and learn while resting. A family group should be able to hike to the top and complete the Ceremonial Trail in two to three hours. No water or toilet facilities can be found along the trail, but they are available at the trailhead or visitor center from May to mid-September.

A park entrance fee is required to enter Bear Butte State Park. A daily permit costs two dollars per person twelve years of age or older. An annual entrance license costs fifteen dollars.

For More Information: Contact Bear Butte State Park, P.O. Box 688, Sturgis, SD 57785, (605) 347-5240.

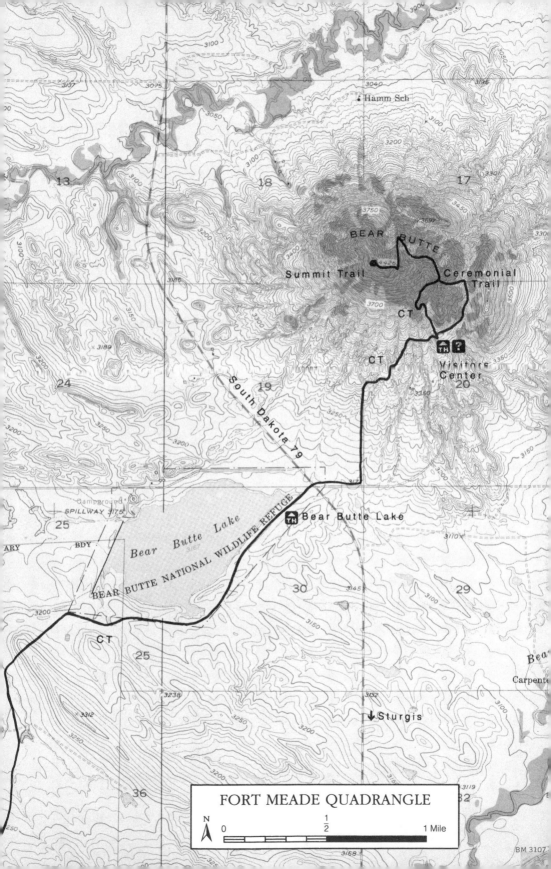

13

18

17

Hamm Sch

BEAR BUTTE

Summit Trail

Ceremonial Trail

CT

CT

Visitors Center

20

24

19

South Dakota 79

25

Campground
SPILLWAY 3175

Bear Butte Lake

BEAR BUTTE NATIONAL WILDLIFE REFUGE

Bear Butte Lake

30

29

25

CT

Bear

Carpente

36

Sturgis

32

FORT MEADE QUADRANGLE

N

0   ½   1 Mile

BM 3107

MT. COOLIDGE/BUTCHER HILL

WIND CAVE NATIONAL PARK AND CUSTER STATE PARK

Rankin Ridge Trail

WIND CAVE NATIONAL PARK

- ▲ **Description:** An easy loop hike to the tower on the highest point in Wind Cave National Park.
- ▲ **General Location:** Thirteen miles north of Hot Springs, South Dakota.
- ▲ **Access:** From Hot Springs, drive north on U.S. 385 to South Dakota 87. Drive north on South Dakota 87 for 5.2 miles then turn east onto the Rankin Ridge Road. Follow the Rankin Ridge Road 0.4 mile to a parking area.
- ▲ **Distance:** A one-mile loop.
- ▲ **Maps:** Wind Cave National Park Hiking Trails; USGS Mt. Coolidge and Wind Cave, South Dakota, 7.5-minute quadrangles.

Rankin Ridge is the most popular trail on the surface of Wind Cave National Park. The trail is short, easy, and suitable for families with small children. There is an interpretive guide for the trail which is keyed to numbered posts along the trail. The guide is excellent for educating yourself and your children about the natural history of the park.

To follow the numbered posts, hike the loop clockwise. The lookout tower is about half way along. Be sure to climb the tower to fully appreciate the view from Rankin Ridge. Beyond the tower, the trail follows the tower access road back to the parking area. The interpretive guide provides details of the ecology of the ponderosa pine forest atop Rankin Ridge and the geology of the granite which forms the ridge.

To the east of Rankin Ridge is Buffalo Gap, a prominent break in the Dakota Hogback ridge that surrounds the Black Hills. In 1823, Jedediah Smith led a party of fur trappers through Buffalo Gap while on the way to South Pass in Wyoming. Five days later, Smith was mauled by a grizzly bear while struggling through Hell Canyon near the current Jewel Cave National Monument. Smith recovered from the attack, but never returned to the Black Hills.

There is also an interpretive guide for the Elk Mountain Trail, which is located next to the Elk Mountain Campground. The *Elk Mountain Trail Guide* focuses on the ecology of the prairie in Wind Cave National Park.

Although Wind Cave has an excellent trail system, the hiking trails will always be a secondary attraction in the park. The National Park Service offers five different tours of the cave in the summer. The Garden of Eden Tour is the shortest, easiest, and best tour for small children. The Fairgrounds Tour highlights the larger rooms found in the cave. The Natural Entrance Tour is the only one which does not access the cave by elevator. The Candlelight Tour lets visitors see the cave as it was before electric lights were installed along the popular cave routes. This tour requires reservations and is limited to groups of ten since it does not follow a paved path.

For the adventurous, there is the caving tour. This four-hour trip visits an undeveloped part of the cave and introduces novices to the basics of safe caving. Special equipment is used as much of the trip involves crawling and wriggling through narrow passages. The trip is offered only once a day in the summer and reservations are needed. The advance planning is well worth the effort because the caving tour is perhaps as spectacular an afternoon as you can spend in the Black Hills.

Nearby Jewel Cave National Monument offers a similar suite of cave tours. Both caves offer fewer tours from Labor Day to Memorial Day, so call ahead for schedules. Year-round temperatures in both caves are about fifty degrees, so many visitors often hike in the cooler mornings and take a cave tour in the afternoon to avoid the summer heat.

For More Information: Contact Wind Cave National Park, Route 1 Box 190, Hot Springs, SD 57747, (605) 745-4600.

Highland Creek–Lookout Point Trails
WIND CAVE NATIONAL PARK

▲ **Description:** A moderate hike through the northern part of Wind Cave National Park.
▲ **General Location:** Eleven miles north of Hot Springs, South Dakota.
▲ **Access:** From the intersection of U.S. 385 and South Dakota 87, turn north on South Dakota 87. Drive 8 miles, nearly to the park boundary, and turn east onto gravel National Park Service Road 5. Drive 1.3 miles to the Centennial Trail–Highland Creek Trailhead and then 1.4 miles farther to the start of the Highland Creek Trail 7.
▲ **Distance:** This hike is 7.8 miles one way. A car shuttle is required, or this route can be combined with the Centennial Trail to form a 14-mile loop.

▲ **Maps:** Wind Cave National Park Hiking Trails; USGS Wind Cave, South Dakota, 7.5-minute quadrangle.

The Centennial Trail and Highland Creek trails form the backbone of the trail system in Wind Cave National Park. Because of its length, Highland Creek is the most diverse trail in the park, traversing prairie, forest, and riparian habitats, as well as a prairie dog town. Combine the Highland Creek and Lookout Point trails to make a superb one-day trip.

From the junction of NPS Road 5 and Trail 7, hike south on an old two-track dirt road. After about one-half mile, begin to descend from the prairie towards the valley of Highland Creek. Cross Highland Creek near a prairie dog town where you may also see bison.

Loop around the north and west sides of two side draws to Highland Creek as the old road follows a crest of a ridge. Descend south from the ridge to reach the junction with Trail 5 in the bottom of a side draw at 3.3 miles. To reach the Centennial Trail turn right and follow Trail 5 northwest for 1.5 miles.

To continue south on the Highland Creek Trail turn left. The trail continues to follow an old two-track road as it climbs to the divide between Highland and Beaver creeks. Reach a corner of the park, turn southwest, and descend into Limestone Canyon. Follow Limestone Canyon a short distance downstream to reach Beaver Creek at 5 miles.

Hike upstream along Beaver Creek making one crossing just before the trail leaves the south side of the valley at 5.4 miles. Climb to a prairie, which is the north limit of Bison Flats. The Highland Creek–Lookout Point Trail junction is at 5.9 miles near a research exclosure in a prairie dog town. Continue west on the Lookout Point Trail as it follows an old road to reach U.S. 87 at 7.8 miles. This junction is 0.2 mile south of the Norbeck Dam–Centennial Trail Trailhead.

Trails 7 and 4 can be combined with the Centennial Trail to form two short loop hikes. Trail 4 and the south end of the Centennial Trail can be combined to form an easy 4.9-mile loop around Beaver Creek. Trails 7, 5, and the Centennial Trail can be combined to form a moderate 6.3-mile loop accessible from two points on NPS Road 5. If you're ambitious, combine Trails 7, 4, and the entire Centennial Trail in Wind Cave National Park to make an overnight hike.

Along the Highland Creek Trail you'll see prairie dogs and bison and will probably see mule deer and elk if you are quiet and careful. Forty species of grasses have been identified in the mixed grass prairie of the park. Blue grama is the most common, and western wheatgrass, little bluestem, and threadleaf sedge are also abundant.

Wind Cave National Park trails generally follow old two-track dirt roads. Consequently, they are normally easy to follow. But the roads are rapidly recovering, and some parts may be difficult to recognize, particularly in prairie dog towns. Most trail junctions are marked with large posts with trail numbers carved in the top. Cross-country travel in the park is easy, so carry your topographic map with you.

To camp overnight in the park you must obtain a free Backcountry Use Permit from either the visitors center or a Centennial Trail access point. All plants, animals, and cultural features in the park are protected and cannot be disturbed. No open fires are allowed and there is no drinking water in the backcountry. Campsites must be located at least one-quarter mile from any maintained roads and must be at least one hundred feet from water sources or archeological sites.

For More Information: Contact Wind Cave National Park, RR 1 Box 190, Hot Springs, SD 57747-9430, (605) 745-4600.

Prairie Trail
CUSTER STATE PARK

▲ **Description:** A short, easy loop hike through the grasslands in the southern part of Custer State Park.
▲ **General Location:** Eighteen miles southeast of Custer, South Dakota.
▲ **Access:** From Custer, drive east on U.S. 16A to South Dakota 87. Turn south on South Dakota 87 and drive 5.8 to the southwest end of the Wildlife Loop Road (Custer State Park Road 1). Drive 4.5 miles east on the Wildlife Loop Road and park at a small lot on the south side of the road.
▲ **Length:** Custer State Park lists the loop as 3.5 miles around, but it is probably closer to 2.5 miles.
▲ **Maps:** Custer State Park Trail Guide; USGS Mt. Coolidge, South Dakota, 7.5-minute quadrangle. An interpretive guide for the Prairie Trail is available from the Peter Norbeck Visitor Center or the Blue Bell Entrance Station.

Most hikers in Custer State Park follow the popular trails which leave from the parking area at Sylvan Lake. For those wishing more solitude, and different terrain, the park offers a variety of short loop trails which are ideal for family outings. The most unusual of these trails is the Prairie Trail.

Our route starts by crossing the valley of the south fork of Lame Johnny Creek, and climbing to Hay Flats. The trail then descends to Flynn Creek before the loop closes just south of the parking area.

The *Custer State Park Interpretive Guide* for the Prairie Trail is an invaluable addition to your hike. The booklet contains useful flower, grass and forb, woody plant, mammal, and bird checklists. Numbered posts along the trail are keyed to specific features which are discussed in the booklet. The trail is marked by these posts and generally follows a well-defined footway. Hikers must climb two fences on stiles. The fences are used to separate winter and summer pastures for the park's bison herd.

The Prairie Trail is an excellent place to study the dry grasslands of the southern Black Hills. Wheatgrass, buffalograss, green needlegrass, bluestems, and gramas are the most common grasses. Scattered groves of ponderosa pine show that the mountain forests have not yielded completely to the plains grasslands. Burr oak, the only oak species native to the Black Hills, is found near Flynn Creek along with green ash and American elm.

"Edge areas," where forests meet grasslands, are biologically very productive. Edge areas are often the best places for observing Custer State Park's diverse wildlife population. Meadowlarks and magpies are common birds seen and heard along the trail. Mule deer, whitetail deer, antelope, raccoon, and coyotes are common in the southern part of the park.

Lucky hikers may spot part of the park's bison or elk herds. Elk will generally flee from people, but bison should be avoided. They are huge, fast, and not always as docile as they appear.

Hikers should be prepared for the grasslands environment. This preparation should include protection from the sun and a good supply of water. Afternoon storms are common; be sure to take cover in the event of lightening, but do use trees for shelter in an electrical storm.

Hikers further interested in the natural history of the Custer State Park can consult *Natural History of the Black Hills and Badlands* by Froiland.

For More Information: Contact Custer State Park, HC 83 Box 70, Custer, SD 57730, (605) 255-4515 or 255-4464 for the Peter Norbeck Visitor Center in summer.

French Creek Natural Area
CUSTER STATE PARK

- ▲ **Description:** A one- or two-day off-trail hike along beautiful French Creek.
- ▲ **General Location:** Ten miles southeast of Custer, South Dakota.
- ▲ **Access:** From Custer, drive east on U.S. 16A. To reach the west trailhead turn south on South Dakota 87 and drive 4.8 miles to Blue Bell Resort. From the resort drive 2.6 miles east on Custer State Park Road 4 to a marked trailhead. To reach the east trailhead, drive east on U.S. 16A to the Wildlife Loop Road and then 3.8 miles south to the trailhead. A car can be left at both ends for a one-way hike. The hike is described west to east, which is downstream.

▲ **Distance:** About 12 miles one way.
▲ **Maps:** Custer State Park Trail Guide; USGS Mt. Coolidge and Butcher Hill, South Dakota, 7.5-minute quadrangles.

Hidden in the center of Custer State Park is the French Creek Natural Area. Twenty-two hundred acres are managed to minimize human impact around the creek and its canyon. A hiking route meanders through woodlands alongside French Creek as the creek cuts through the eastern slope of the Black Hills to reach the grasslands beyond.

This is a much different hike than trips on the maintained trails in Custer State Park. As a day hike, the trip can take up to eight hours. French Creek is one of the few hikes in South Dakota that is commonly done as an overnight backpack trip. Designated campsites for overnight stays are located near each end of the trail. The route through French Creek is not maintained between the two campsites. However, the route is obvious in most places and not difficult to follow until the narrows are reached.

Permits are necessary for overnight camping and can be obtained at the Peter Norbeck Visitor Center. The fee is one dollar a night and there is a limit of fifteen people per night, per campsite. Advance reservations are accepted, but not required. Camping is allowed only in the designated campsites and fires must be confined to established fire grates at the campsites. Water from the creek must be treated before drinking. Poison ivy is very common along the route, and prairie rattlesnakes are occasionally sighted.

The French Creek narrows are the highlight of the trip and easily the wildest area in Custer State Park. There is just enough challenge in walking and scrambling among the granite boulders to make the mouth of the narrows a little intimidating for hikers inexperienced at travelling off trail. Working your way downstream alongside steep cliff walls without any sign of previous hikers gives one a feeling of exploration that is rare in the Black Hills. High water may require that the narrows be bypassed by climbing up the steep canyon walls and following the creek from the plateaus above. At lower water, hikers can follow along or in the creek, stopping occasionally to refresh themselves in some of the larger pools of water. A wide, steel aqueduct on a trestle above the canyon marks the normal limit of summer stream flow. Downstream, the water runs underground when it reaches permeable sedimentary rocks.

Horseback riders use the western part of French Creek. There is a well-defined footway on the western side until Horse Trail 1 leaves French Creek Canyon to climb to the north rim at Lockwood Springs. Horseback riders are restricted to the marked trail in the Natural Area.

Wildlife watching is another attraction of this walk. Bighorn sheep, elk, and occasionally bison can be seen along the French Creek. On one spring attempt to bypass the narrows, a friend and I came upon a newborn mountain goat kid and its mother. The kid wobbled as it tried to walk and still had its umbilical cord attached. We took a few quick pictures and left the pair in peace. French Creek is also noted for excellent bird watching and trout fishing. Bird species along French Creek include the lazuli bunting, black-and-white warbler, and western tanager. Brook, brown, and rainbow trout live in French Creek.

The first documented discovery of gold in the Black Hills was made along French Creek by miners with Custer's 1874 Black Hills Expedition. The diggings near the present town of Custer never amounted to much, but word of the find triggered a gold rush throughout the Black Hills. It is ironic that French Creek is now one of the few areas in the Black Hills to be managed as a wild area and that the only sign of mining activity is a small tunnel driven into pegmatite.

For More Information: Contact Custer State Park, HC 83 Box 70, Custer, SD 57730, (605) 255-4415 or 255-4464 for the Peter Norbeck Visitor Center in summer.

Lovers Leap Trail
CUSTER STATE PARK

▲ **Description:** A short loop trail suitable for family groups which leads to a spectacular overlook above Galena Creek.
▲ **General Location:** Ten miles east of Custer, South Dakota.
▲ **Access:** From Custer drive east on U.S. 16A to Custer State Park. Continue east on U.S. 16A to the Peter Norbeck Visitor Center. One-tenth of a mile east of the visitor center there is a parking area beside an old schoolhouse on the south side of the road. The trail begins beyond a sign, in the woods to the southeast.
▲ **Distance:** 4-mile loop, moderately difficult.
▲ **Maps:** Custer State Park Trail Guide; USGS Iron Mountain, South Dakota, 7.5-minute quadrangle.

The massive granite cliffs above Galena Creek are the site of a Native American legend about two young lovers who leapt to their deaths from the cliffs. Today, hikers follow the popular Lovers Leap Trail to the cliffs for less compelling reasons. They are drawn by the spectacular views to the north of Harney Peak, the Needles, and the Cathedral Spires, and by the beautiful, quiet walk along Galena Creek.

The trail begins by climbing steeply along switchbacks to a ridge high above Grace Coolidge Creek. Don't panic, this is the only difficult part of the hike. Once on the ridge, the trail follows an old jeep trail west to a short side trail which leads to the overlook at Lovers Leap. From Lovers Leap, the trail continues to follow the ridge which now trends southwest. A steep descent then brings hikers alongside Galena Creek. After crossing Galena Creek many times, the trail merges with a road along an unnamed tributary of Galena Creek. The gravel road leads to the Coolidge Inn. From the inn a walkway leads past the park chapel back to the old schoolhouse.

The trail is easy to follow. The footway is well worn and marked by black arrows set in orange blazes. There is no drinking water along the route, so carry water along with your lunch.

The Lovers Leap Trail is short and diverse enough to be suitable for family groups. The only difficult part is the climb at the beginning. The ridge-line hiking that follows is particularly scenic. The ponderosa-pine-dominated forest along the ridge is typical of Custer State Park. The west side of the ridge was burned in the 1988 Galena fire. The fire began on July 4, 1988, and burned out of control for five days. Over sixteen thousand acres and $4.4 million worth of timber were lost in the blaze. Over one thousand fire fighters fought the blaze, but it was not controlled until a large rain and hail storm doused the area. Damage from the fire is visible along the trail and from Lovers Leap. There is a small logging operation where the trail turns off the ridge to descend to Galena Creek.

The final section of trail along Galena Creek is cool and shaded from the sun. There are no holes large enough for swimming, but hikers can use the many creek crossings to look for small brook trout. You may see red-tailed hawks from the trail or belted kingfishers by Galena Creek.

For More Information: Contact Custer State Park, HC 83 Box 70, Custer, SD 57730, (605) 255-4515 or 255-4464 for the Peter Norbeck Visitor Center in summer.

Sunday Gulch Trail
CUSTER STATE PARK

▲ **Description:** A short loop trail which descends into Sunday Gulch then ascends along a ridge to the west.
▲ **General Location:** At Sylvan Lake, six miles north of Custer, South Dakota.
▲ **Access:** From Custer, drive 6.3 miles north on U.S. 89, turn east onto U.S. 87, then drive 0.3 mile to the Sylvan Lake parking area. From Hill City, drive

3 miles south to the junction of U.S. 385 and 87. Turn east on U.S. 87 and after 6.1 miles reach the parking area at Sylvan Lake.

▲ **Distance:** About a 3½-mile-long loop. The sign at the start of the loop reads "3 miles," and the Black Hills National Forest lists the trail as 5 miles.

▲ **Maps:** Black Hills National Forest; Custer State Park Trail Guide; Sierra Club Hiking Map of the Norbeck Wildlife Preserve; USGS Custer, South Dakota, 7.5-minute quadrangle.

Three trails leave Custer State Park's most popular trailhead at Sylvan Lake. The two most popular lead east and north to Harney Peak. A less-travelled route leads west down into Sunday Gulch. This streamside route explores a vastly different landscape than the trails to the east.

From the parking area, follow the Sylvan Lakeshore Trail to a point just below the Sylvan Lake Dam where the Sunday Gulch loop begins by a prominent trail sign. The trail begins with a steep descent down the boulder-strewn canyon of Sunday Gulch. Concrete steps and handrails make the descent of the upper canyon easier. As the trail descends further into the gulch, hikers pass through a diverse forest of ponderosa pine, white spruce, paper birch, and quaking aspen which are supported by the cool, moist environment along the stream.

At the low point of the route, the trail turns southwest and begins a steady climb. A short stretch of the trail skirts the shoulder of U.S. 87 before it reenters the woods. The final section of trail passes behind Sylvan Lake Lodge before the loop closes at Sylvan Lake Dam. Remember not to cross U.S. 87 and to pass behind Sylvan Lake Lodge. Hike downhill between some granite boulders to return to the Sylvan Lakeshore Trail. Hikers can return to the parking area via the north half of the Sylvan Lakeshore Trail.

Custer State Park publishes an interpretive guide for the trail which is available at the Peter Norbeck Visitor Center and the Sylvan Lake Entrance Station. The guide contains useful bird, mammal, flower, and woody plant checklists. Discussions of the natural history of the area are keyed to numbered posts along the route. The guide is an excellent introduction to the area, and should be obtained by anyone planning to hike the route.

Custer State Park supports a small population of mountain goats, some of which may be seen from the trail. Whitetail deer are common along the trail and brook trout may be seen in the stream.

The area below the Sylvan Lake Dam is one of the most popular rock climbing areas in the Black Hills. The spires directly behind the dam are known as "the outlets." Below the outlets lies "Middle Earth," where the spires, walls, and climbing routes derive their names from the J. R. R. Tolkien trilogy *Lord of the Rings*.

No drinking water is available on the route, but there is a small store at Sylvan Lake which is open in summer. Poison ivy grows along the trail and is especially common in spring and early summer. Avoid any plants with the distinctive cluster of three shiny leaves. The stream and much of the trail in Sunday Gulch is frozen from late fall through early spring, making for very difficult hiking.

For More Information: Contact Custer State Park, HC 83 Box 70, Custer, SD 57730, (605) 255-4515 or 255-4464 for the Peter Norbeck Visitor Center in summer.

Little Devils Tower Trail
CUSTER STATE PARK

▲ **Description:** A short hike to one of the most spectacular overlooks in the Norbeck Wildlife Preserve.
▲ **General Location:** Seven miles northeast of Custer, South Dakota.
▲ **Access:** From Sylvan Lake, drive about three-quarters mile east on South Dakota 87 to the Little Devils Tower parking area on the north side of the highway.
▲ **Distance:** 3 miles round trip.
▲ **Maps:** Black Hills National Forest; Custer State Park Trail Guide; Sierra Club Hiking Map of the Norbeck Wildlife Preserve; USGS Custer, South Dakota, 7.5-minute quadrangle.

Most of the hiking trails in the Norbeck Wildlife Preserve are long, and difficult at best, for families with small children. The exception is the Little Devils Tower Trail, which is short, but requires a steep climb at the end. However, the rewards at the summit far outweigh the effort spent on the climb. From the top you can see Harney Peak and rugged ridges which extend east above Nelson Creek. The tower has perhaps the best views of the Cathedral Spires and Needles, both close by to the south. Sylvan Peak is prominent to the west, and much of the Norbeck trail system is visible. At night the stars and the lights of Rapid City are especially impressive.

Start from the Little Devils Tower parking area, and hike east on the Cathedral Spires Trail 4. The trail follows the north side of a creek through a forest of spruce, birch, aspen, and willow. Reach a signed junction and take the left fork to the tower while the right fork, and Trail 4, continue to the Cathedral Spires.

There are fewer blazes beyond the junction, but the footway is well defined as the trail stays on the north side of the valley. Pass an old fence which ends on the south side of the trail. Begin to climb steadily beyond the fence. Just before reaching a divide, look for a red arrow painted onto a blaze in a tree. The arrow marks a cleft between two granite monoliths. Exit the cleft uphill and follow more painted arrows up to, and about twenty feet beyond, a narrow divide. Follow arrows painted on rocks through another cleft and then up a route which scrambles to the summit. Return by retracing your route. Little Devils Tower can also be combined with the Harney Peak–Sylvan Lake loop described in this guide.

The scrambling at the end of the climb will be difficult for smaller children, but this section is very short. Once on top, be sure to pay attention where you step. The drop-off of the north face is every bit as vertical as the one at the "big" Devils Tower.

For More Information: Contact Custer State Park, HC 83 Box 70, Custer, SD 57730, (605) 255-4515 or 255-4464 for the Peter Norbeck Visitor Center in summer.

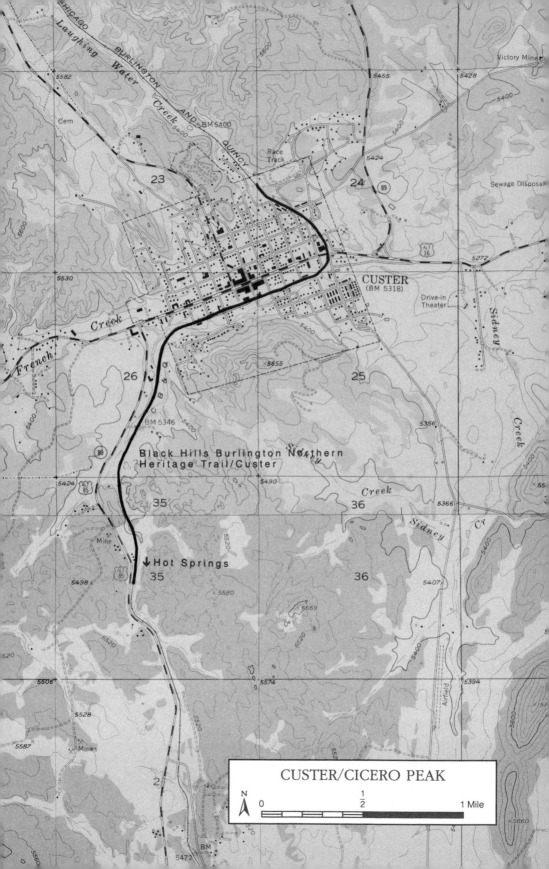

CUSTER/CICERO PEAK

BLACK HILLS
SOUTH DAKOTA

Black Hills Burlington
Northern Heritage Trail
CUSTER PROJECT

▲ **Description:** An easy hike or bike ride through the town of Custer.
▲ **General Location:** The trail starts in Custer, South Dakota, and extends south of town.
▲ **Access:** From the junction of U.S. 16 and 16A in Custer drive one block south, nearly to the railroad grade, and then one block east to the parking area at Harbach Centennial Park.
▲ **Distance:** 2.6 miles of trail is complete.
▲ **Maps:** USGS Custer and Cicero Peak, South Dakota, 7.5-minute quadrangles.

October 3, 1992, was another milestone for South Dakota's rails to trails project. On that day the late Governor George Mickelson dedicated the second section of the Black Hills Burlington Northern Heritage Trail and the Custer City Parkway and Recreation Trail. The governor strongly supported the trail project because it gives everyone a chance to enjoy the Black Hills at a time when public access to the outdoors is being limited. Mickelson felt that the recreation aspect of the trail is as important as the arrival of railroads was to the Black Hills one hundred years ago. His support of the project earned the governor a special citation from former Interior Secretary Manuel Lujan for fostering growth of outdoor recreation. The opening of this section of trail comes on the heels of a ruling by the South Dakota Supreme Court which upheld the right of the state to use the abandoned railway as a foot trail.

To see the trail for yourself, try a trip north or south along the trail from Harbach Park. To the north, the trail extends 0.9 mile to the Custer

High School athletic fields near the city limit. This is an "urban" trail section, crossing many city streets and U.S. 16A.

To the south, the trail leads 0.3 mile south to near the Chief Motel where a gate blocks vehicles from using the trail. Once out of town the trail is quieter, but still never gets too far from U.S. 385. After 1.7 miles the trail ends at a point just south of the Gray Rocks Resort.

Like the demonstration project near Lead, this section of trail has been covered with a layer of compacted gravel. Signs at both ends urge users not to venture onto unopened trail sections, both for their own safety and to avoid damaging already difficult relations with adjacent landowners. The trail will eventually connect Custer with Deadwood to the north and Edgemont to the south.

Driving through Custer one sees only its present—a town dependent on the motels, gift shops, and restaurants of the tourist trade. The railroad grade allows you to see Custer's past as you pass the plants which processed and shipped pegmatite minerals from the many mines around town.

For More Information: Contact the South Dakota Department of Game, Fish, and Parks, 523 E. Capitol, Pierre, SD 57501, (605) 773-3391; or the Black Hills Rails to Trails Association, Box 777 South Junction Ave., Sturgis, SD 57785, (605) 347-3604.

Harney Peak–Sylvan Lake Trails
BLACK HILLS NATIONAL FOREST

▲ **Description:** A moderate loop hike to the top of Harney Peak, the highest point in South Dakota, and a return leg through the Cathedral Spires.
▲ **General Location:** Nine miles north of Custer, South Dakota.
▲ **Access:** From Hill City, drive 3 miles south to the junction of U.S. 385 and U.S. 87. Turn east onto South Dakota 87 and drive 6.1 miles to reach Sylvan Lake. Park in the day-use area located just past the parking area at Sylvan Lake. The trail starts at the northwest corner of the day-use loop road, next to a large trail sign. From Custer, drive 6.3 miles north on U.S. 89, turn east on U.S. 87, then drive 0.3 mile to reach Sylvan Lake.
▲ **Distance:** 7 miles round trip, including the Cathedral Spires on the return leg.
▲ **Maps:** Black Hills National Forest; Sierra Club Hiking Map of the Norbeck Wildlife Preserve; USGS Custer, South Dakota, 7.5-minute quadrangle.

Harney Peak is the highest point in South Dakota, and a popular goal for all Black Hills hikers. The peak can be reached from any one of

CUSTER/HILL CITY QUADRANGLES

N

0   1/2   1 Mile

Willow Creek
Horse CG

BM 5195

Hill City
7   8

Cross-country
Route

Palmer

Elk

Nelson Creek

Willow Creek

Harney Peak Trails

Grizzly Bear
Mine

5492

6000

18   17   16

18   17   16

Nelson Creek

6482

6810

6527

Harney Peak

Lookout Tower

Gap Lode Mine

6200

6485

19   20   21

6727

6712

6800

Sunday
Gulch
Trail

6405

6426

Sylvan Lake
Shore Trail

Little Devils Tower

30

Little Devils Tower Trail

Cathedral Spires

Sylvan Lake

28

TH

87

Needle Eye

Custer

89

eleven trailheads which surround the Black Elk Wilderness and Norbeck Wildlife Preserve, but by far the most popular route is via Sylvan Lake. Adventurous hikers can make a loop via the Cathedral Spires, the most spectacular of the granite pinnacles which surround Harney Peak.

From the trail sign at the northwest corner of the day-use area, hike about a hundred feet on the Sylvan Lakeshore Trail before turning north onto Trail 9, the Sylvan Lake–Harney Trail. It is a three-mile climb from the lake to the summit on Trail 9. From the lake, climb steadily to a junction with the south fork of the Lost Cabin Trail 2, then turn east onto a gentle ridge which offers good views to the north.

Immediately after crossing into the Black Elk Wilderness, Trail 9 reaches a junction with the east fork of Trail 2 at the site of the Midway Picnic Ground. Trail 9 continues east at a moderate grade to reach a junction with Trail 4, and then 0.1 mile farther a junction with Trail 7. Trail 7 leads five miles east to Mount Rushmore.

Continue on Trail 9 as it resumes a steady climb and gains over 600 feet in less than a mile. Turn off Trail 9 at the summit junction, climb over a small ridge and navigate a maze of trails to the tower on top of Harney Peak.

The view from Harney Peak may be the finest in the Black Hills. To the east lies Rapid City and Ellsworth Air Force Base. Off in the distance is Badlands National Park. To the north, beyond Hill City, are Custer Peak, Terry Peak, and Bear Butte. On the west side are Bear Mountain and the high Limestone Plateau. Odakota Mountain, at 7,200 feet on the plateau, is the second highest point in South Dakota. To the south is Mount Coolidge, the highest point in Custer State Park, and closer to the peak are the Needles, Cathedral Spires, and Little Devils Tower.

To complete a loop back to Sylvan Lake, retrace Trail 9 back to the junction with the Cathedral Spires Trail 4. Follow Trail 4 south to a junction with Trail 3, the Willow Creek–Rushmore Trail, which is about a mile from the peak. Continue on Trail 4 a short distance to reach the north side of the Cathedral Spires.

The spires are actually a series of vertical slabs with highpoints on their northwest sides. The summits are numbered 1 through 9 from west to east. All are technical rock climbs. Spire 4 is the highest, and Spire 5 is the easiest to climb. Mountain goats have been sighted on the top of Spire 5. Custer's 1874 expedition originally named the spires the "Organ Pipes."

After passing between the spires and the "Picket Fence," which is the group of spires to the north of the trail, Trail 4 forks. The south fork leads between the spires and the spectacular wall of Bartizan to the Needles Highway (South Dakota 87). Limber pine, an uncommon species in the Black Hills, occurs between the split in Trail 4 and the Needles Highway.

To complete the loop, follow the west fork which passes a side trail to Little Devils Tower before reaching a different parking area on the Needles Highway. Hike through the parking area, and follow Trail 4 for one-half mile before reaching the day-use area at Sylvan Lake.

Harney Peak is roughly the center of a large outcrop of granite of Precambrian Age. Granite weathers and erodes to form the spectacular needles and spires common in the area between Sylvan Lake and the Needles Highway. Associated with the granite is an especially coarse-grained form called pegmatite, which contains crystals ranging in size from inches to feet. Pegmatites also concentrate rare elements such as lithium and beryllium which are mined along with the more common minerals feldspar, rose quartz, and mica from numerous mines in pegmatite around Keystone and Custer.

The Norbeck trails are among the best marked and maintained in the Black Hills. Trails are marked with blazes which may have the trail number carved in the center. The loop described here is heavily used and the trails are deeply eroded in some spots. Horseback riding is permitted on most trails and mountain bikes are allowed on all trails outside the Black Elk Wilderness and Mount Rushmore. Camping in the area does not require a permit.

Harney Peak receives less snow than the northern Black Hills, so year-round hiking is possible for the hardy. Sandy soils formed by weathering of granite drain quickly, so the trails are often dry while the roads and trails in the northern Black Hills are still muddy.

For More Information: Contact Custer Ranger District, 330 Mount Rushmore Road, Custer, SD 57730, (605) 673-4853; or Custer State Park, HC 83 Box 70, Custer, SD 57730, (605) 255-4515.

Harney Peak–Willow Creek Trails
BLACK HILLS NATIONAL FOREST

▲ **Description:** A long hike to the top of Harney Peak from the north side.
▲ **General Location:** Six miles east of Hill City, South Dakota.
▲ **Access:** From Hill City, drive 3 miles south to the junction of U.S. 16 and South Dakota 244. Follow South Dakota 244 east for 3 miles to a sign for the Willow Creek Horse Camp. Turn south onto the gravel road and park at the day-use area which is located just before the horse camp.
▲ **Distance:** 10 miles round trip, with 2,200 feet of elevation gain.
▲ **Maps:** Black Hills National Forest; Sierra Club Hiking Map of the Norbeck Wildlife Preserve; USGS Hill City and Custer, South Dakota, 7.5-minute quadrangles.

My favorite route up Harney Peak starts from the north side. The trailhead at Willow Creek is closer to the northern Black Hills and Rapid City, and thus is more convenient than the Sylvan Lake approach. Fewer people use the north approach and you may have the trail to yourself until you reach the summit. The route is also more scenic, but more importantly, the increase in distance and elevation gain on the north side give Harney the feel of a much larger mountain.

The route is simple and easy to follow. From Willow Creek take Harney–Sylvan Lake Trail 9 to the east shoulder of the peak and then follow a short spur trail to the summit lookout. The north end of Trail 9 is the least interesting part of the trip. Here Trail 9 follows an old dirt road, which is parallel to South Dakota 244, to a junction with Trail 8 at 0.9 mile. Climb steadily away from the road to a junction with Trail 5 at 1.8 miles. Beyond the junction with Trail 5, the trail enters the Black Elk Wilderness and leaves the road behind.

Once into the wilderness, cross a small spring and hike among the impressive granite spires which form the southwest side of Elkhorn Mountain. A small knob just beyond Elkhorn Mountain offers a spectacular view of the backside of Mount Rushmore. From the knob, Trail 9 follows the open northeast ridge of Harney Peak at a gentle grade to reach 6,800 feet. From this point, Trail 9 climbs steadily on switchbacks to the summit lookout tower.

A small spring on the northwest side of Elkhorn Mountain marks the start of an alternate off-trail route to return to Willow Creek Horse Camp. Bushwack alongside a branch of Willow Creek for about a half mile to the confluence with the main stem of Willow Creek. A dam completely filled by sediment is located near the confluence. Two short spur trails lead from the dam to Trail 8 (Willow Creek Trail). Follow Trail 8 west to Trail 2 and then back to the trailhead. Hikers should be cautious on this trail, as it is the most popular horse trail in Norbeck.

Harney Peak was named for General William S. Harney in 1857 by members of an early military expedition led by Kemble Warren and the renowned geologist Ferdinand V. Hayden. The first attempt to climb the peak was made by part of Custer's 1874 expedition. Like many parties to follow them, Custer's group ran out of daylight just below the summit, and was forced to abandon their attempt. The Custer expedition was successful in leaving their mark on the geography of the Black Hills, naming both Custer Peak, for their leader, and Terry Peak, for General Alfred H. Terry.

Numerous prehistoric ascents of Harney were undoubtedly made by Native Americans. In 1875, Dr. Valentine T. McGillycuddy was part of the Jenney Scientific Expedition to the Black Hills and made the first recorded ascent by a white man. Dr. McGillycuddy's ashes now rest at the base of the steps in the lookout tower. The tower was completed shortly before the doctor's death and was manned as a fire lookout from 1938 to 1967. The tower stands as a monument to both depression-era construction workers, and the fire lookouts who followed. The tower was placed on the National Register of Historic Places in 1982.

The Harney Peak area has long been a focus of conservation efforts. Peter Norbeck, who was later to become governor and United States senator from South Dakota, was instrumental in creating Custer State Forest, which later became Custer State Park. The Norbeck Wildlife Refuge was created in 1920 to protect game animals and birds and to provide a breeding place for them. Norbeck's conservation legacy also includes the creation of Grand Teton and Badlands national parks.

In 1980, Congress created the 9,824-acre Black Elk Wilderness which protects the heart of the Norbeck Wildlife Preserve. The legislation came about, at least in part, due to opposition to a proposal to build an aerial tramway from Keystone, near Mount Rushmore, to the top of Harney Peak. Currently, ten thousand acres in Norbeck have been proposed as additions to the Black Elk Wilderness despite Black Hills National Forest plans for massive logging efforts in the preserve.

For More Information: Contact Custer Ranger District, 330 Mount Rushmore Road, Custer, SD 57730, (605) 673-4853.

Norbeck East Trails Loop
BLACK HILLS NATIONAL FOREST

▲ **Description:** A one- or two-day hike through the east side of the Black Elk Wilderness and Norbeck Wildlife Preserve.

▲ **General Location:** Three miles south of Keystone, South Dakota.

▲ **Access:** From Keystone drive 1 mile south on U.S. 16A. Turn east onto South Dakota 244 and drive 1.8 miles to Mount Rushmore National Memorial. The unmarked Mount Rushmore Trailhead is located south of the parking area across South Dakota 244. Look for a trail leading up from the east end of the guardrail along the road.

▲ **Distance:** About 12 miles.

▲ **Maps:** Sierra Club Hiking Map of the Norbeck Wildlife Preserve; Black Hills National Forest Norbeck Wildlife Preserve and Black Elk Wilderness Trail System; and USGS Custer, Hill City, Iron Mountain, and Mt. Rushmore, South Dakota, 7.5-minute quadrangles.

The eastern side of the Norbeck Wildlife Preserve contains some of the most scenic areas in the Black Hills. None of the famous granite spires are here, but a less-known group which extends southwest from

Horsethief Lake is nearly as impressive as the Needles or Cathedral Spires. Many hikers will savor the streamside sections of trails along Grizzly Bear and Iron creeks.

A loop extending west from Mount Rushmore along trails 3, 5, 14, and 7 covers most of the northeast part of the preserve. This hike can be done in one long day, but is better as an easy overnight hike.

From the parking area at Mount Rushmore, hike south down Trail 3 for one-half mile to the boundary of the Black Elk Wilderness. Just beyond the boundary, cross a side draw of Grizzly Bear Creek and come to the junction with Trail 5 which is also part of the Centennial Trail here. (This trail may still be labeled as Trail 10.) Turn right onto Trail 5, cross a corner of the Mount Rushmore National Memorial, and hike north to the former junction with Trail 10. Trail 10 was abandoned by the Forest Service in early 1992 because it crosses prime mountain goat breeding grounds.

Beyond the junction with Trail 10, continue north on Trail 5 to a junction with Trail 14 at a spectacular group of granite spires. Turn south onto Trail 14 to hike alongside the spires. After crossing through the spires, reach a junction with Trail 7 in the valley of Grizzly Bear Creek. Several good campsites can be found on the high ground above the beaver dams which flood the valley. This is a good midway point of the trip for groups planning an overnight hike.

From the Trail 14-7 junction, hike southeast on Trail 7 past the western end of abandoned Trail 10. Cross over a divide into the drainage of Iron Creek. After about one mile, leave the Black Elk Wilderness where the trail becomes a two-track dirt road. Trail 7 has been recently relocated to follow this road for 1.1 miles to the intersection of Trails 3 and 15 just west of a prominent granite tower. From this point to the junction with Trail 5, Trail 3 is part of the Centennial Trail.

Turn northeast onto Trail 3 and hike for 0.6 mile to a four-way junction with Trail 16 and BHNF Road 347. Continue north on Trail 3 for 1.1 miles to the Black Elk Wilderness boundary, then over the divide and into the Grizzly Bear Creek drainage back to Mount Rushmore.

The Black Hills National Forest plans some major changes for the Norbeck trail system in the next few years. Current efforts focus on developing a bypass around the Black Elk Wilderness so that mountain bikes have an uninterrupted route through the forest on the Centennial Trail. Mountain bikes are illegal in designated wilderness areas, and therefore not allowed on the Centennial Trail in the Black Elk Wilderness. Other trails in Norbeck will be relocated to move the trails off roads and away from areas prone to flooding by beaver dams.

Despite the changes planned for the trail systems, the existing trails are well marked and easy to follow. A number of loop trips are possible in addition to the one described here. Several are suitable for overnight trips, in fact the area is ideal for novice backpackers. Campsites in Norbeck must be at least one hundred feet from trails or streams. Giardia is found in the Black Hills, so be sure to treat all your water by boiling or filtering with a filter designed to remove giardia bacteria. Camp stoves are allowed, but open fires are not due to high fire danger.

For More Information: Contact Custer Ranger District, 330 Mount Rushmore Road, Custer, SD 57730, (605) 673-4853.

"Sylvan Peak"
BLACK HILLS NATIONAL FOREST

▲ **Description:** A rugged off-trail hike to the top of an unnamed 7,000-foot peak.
▲ **General Location:** Six miles south of Hill City, South Dakota.
▲ **Access:** From Hill City, drive 3 miles south on U.S. 16. Turn east onto U.S. 87 and drive 3 miles to a prominent left turn where Johnson Canyon crosses the road. Park at a turnout just beyond the next right turn. The route is unmarked, but begins on the slope southwest of the turnout.
▲ **Distance:** 3½-mile round trip with a 1,400-foot climb.
▲ **Maps:** Black Hills National Forest; USGS Custer, South Dakota, 7.5-minute quadrangle.

From the top of Harney Peak you can see most of the Black Hills. Secure with its place as South Dakota's highest point, Harney Peak offers a glimpse of most of the state's other 7,000-footers including Terry Peak, Bear Mountain, Odakota Mountain, and the large area of the Limestone Plateau which climbs over the 7,000-foot mark. But often confused with Bear Mountain, or simply overlooked, is a small range to the west that is bounded by U.S. 16 and 89, and anchored by Buckhorn Mountain on the south and St. Elmo Peak to the north.

The high point of this range checks in at an even 7,000 feet, making it the seventh highest peak in South Dakota. By a quirk of geography, it has never received an official name, so we call it "Sylvan Peak" due its proximity to Sylvan Lake.

There is no trail to the top, but access to the area is possible from anywhere on Black Hills National Forest land from U.S. 87. However, the north ridge of the peak is the most prominent. A start near the mouth of

Johnson Canyon requires an elevation gain of 1,400 feet, one of the largest required to reach any summit in the Black Hills. This obvious and challenging route is entirely on Black Hills National Forest land.

From the turnout, hike southwest to gain the north ridge at an elevation of 6,000 feet. Continue due south on the crest of the ridge, cross an old logging road and reach the north sub-peak at 6,880 feet. It is the cliffs on this sub-peak that appear to be the summit when viewed from near Sylvan Lake. The scramble to the top of the rocky sub-peak is well worth the effort. There are excellent views of Sylvan Lake and Harney Peak. The group of spires around the dam at Sylvan Lake, called the "outlets," are especially prominent.

Cross another old logging road in the saddle between the north and main peaks, and continue southeast to the summit. The lack of a summit cairn or marker post on top indicate that this peak is rarely climbed.

"Sylvan Peak" is a difficult climb, not recommended for hikers unfamiliar with travelling off trail. A topographic map and compass, along with the ability to use these tools, are essential for route finding. There is a lot of fallen timber on the north ridge, and some easy scrambling may be necessary. Hikers looking for a little added adventure in their Black Hills hikes will find these qualities attractive rather than discouraging.

For More Information: Contact Harney Ranger District, HCR 87 Box 51, Hill City, SD 57745, (605) 574-2534.

Bear Mountain Trails
BLACK HILLS NATIONAL FOREST

▲ **Description:** A long cross-country ski or mountain bike loop over the third highest point in South Dakota.

▲ **General Location:** Twelve miles southwest of Hill City, South Dakota.

▲ **Access:** To reach the Medicine Mountain Boy Scout Camp from Hill City, drive 1.3 miles south on U.S. 385 to Pennington County Road T317, which is also called BHNF Road 303 or the Reno Gulch Road. Turn west on T317 which is paved for about a mile. After 9.8 miles, turn left onto BHNF Road 297. Follow Road 297 for 1.6 miles, then turn right onto BHNF Road 299. Reach the Medicine Mountain Boy Scout Camp 1.8 miles later. Drive through the gate and park beside a trail sign in a small lot on the left side of the entrance road. The road is plowed in winter to the scout camp via Medicine Mountain.

▲ **Distance:** The Bear Mountain loop is 9.5 miles long. It is 2.75 miles one way from the Boy Scout Camp to the summit of Bear Mountain.

▲ **Maps:** Black Hills National Forest; USGS Medicine Mountain, Ditch Creek, Signal Hill, and Berne, South Dakota, 7.5-minute quadrangles.

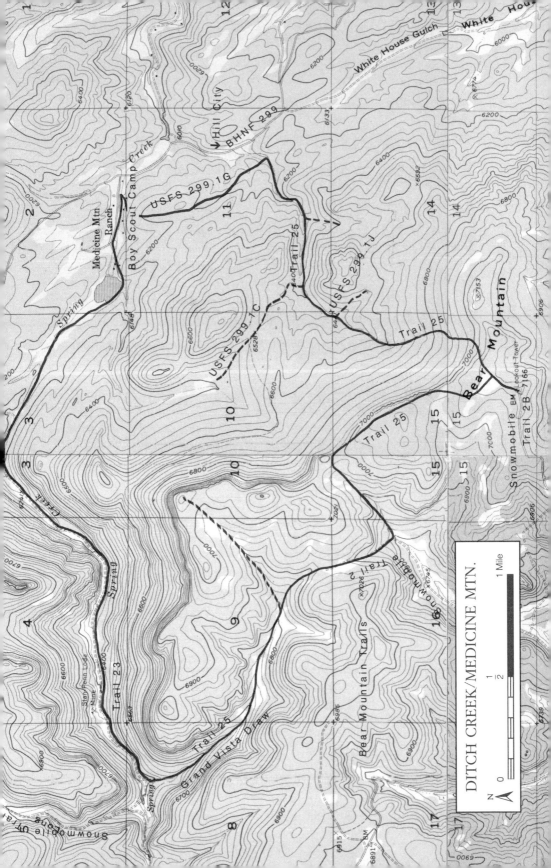

DITCH CREEK/MEDICINE MTN.

Anchoring the northern end of the Bear Mountain trails is Odakota Mountain (7,200 feet), the second highest point in South Dakota. Merely the highest point on the highest ridge of the Limestone Plateau, Odakota, and the views from it, are unimpressive. Bear Mountain (7,166 feet) at the south end of the trail system is the third highest point in the state, and a much more interesting summit.

There is a network of cross-country ski trails around Bear Mountain. The best of these trails can be combined to form a long loop which includes the top of Bear Mountain. Trail 25 leaves the scout camp by heading west through a meadow and then turning south to pass through a gate in a fence. Keep a close eye on the carsonite posts which mark the route here, or ask the scout camp caretaker if you have problems finding the start of the trail. Trail 25 is a narrow, winding hiking trail until it merges with BHNF Road 299.1G.

Follow Road 299.1G until it reaches a prominent draw, then turn west up the draw onto BHNF Road 299.1C. Pass Trail 25B, which is a side trail leading south, and stay left on 299.1J at a fork where 299.1C leads right. Continue straight at another fork where Trail 25B and 299.1J go left. The climb up Bear Mountain begins in earnest from this junction.

Trail 25 steepens considerably and adds a few switchbacks before reaching the summit ridge of Bear Mountain. Once on the ridge, a side road merges from the left and you then pass a gate in an open meadow. From the gate, follow the main road to the Bear Mountain Lookout Tower.

The summit rocks are the same massive limestone that forms the plateau, but Bear Mountain is the center of an uplift of Archean Age granite and gneiss, some of the oldest rocks in the Black Hills.

The lookout tower is closed in winter and views from it are limited. When open, views from the tower extend north and south along the rim of the Limestone Plateau and east to Harney Peak. A well-used spur from Snowmobile Trail 2 reaches the tower, and there are also restrooms adjacent it.

Return to the gate and Trail 25. The section of trail beyond the gate follows the rim of the Limestone Plateau. This is perhaps the most scenic section of ski trail in the Black Hills. There are several spectacular overlooks with views extending east to Harney Peak. The trail winds through open timber and can be difficult to find. If in doubt, just remember that the trail stays very close to the rim.

After about a mile on the rim, Trail 25 turns west near some slash piles, then follows a fence downhill into Grand Vista Draw and a forest service road. From this point to Spring Creek, skiers and snowmobilers share the same route as Cross-country Ski Trail 25 coincides with

Snowmobile Trail 2. For a reprise of the views from the rim of the Limestone Plateau, ski side-trail 25A and Snowmobile Trail 2-P for 0.75 mile northeast to the Grand Vista Overlook.

At the junction with Spring Creek, turn east down Trail 23, while Trail 25 and Snowmobile Trail 2 continue north. Enjoy some well-deserved downhill skiing as Trail 23 follows Spring Creek east. Cross a fence, and about 200 yards later reach an intersection with Trail 21, which enters from the north. Past this intersection the trails are not marked and skiers are on their own back to the scout camp. Just follow Spring Creek and stay to the south side of the large pond, just upstream from the camp.

There is much less snow at Bear Mountain than in the Lead–Deadwood area. Don't be surprised if there is little snow at the scout camp, snow conditions improve markedly with elevation. Nevertheless, keep in mind the option of skiing from BHNF Road 301 south along Long Draw to Odakota Mountain and Spring Creek. This area is higher and holds snow well into the spring. As a last resort, consider hiking up Bear Mountain from the scout camp.

Bear Mountain is not a trip for beginners. Trail markers are sparse and the ability to use a topographic map is a necessity. The loop along Trails 23 and 25 is long and snow conditions may be poor. But for skiers willing to make a little extra effort to climb Bear Mountain or Odakota Mountain via routes away from the snowmobile trail, this area provides an exciting alternative to the easier, and more reliable trails at Big Hill and Eagle Cliff.

In summer, Bear Mountain is excellent for mountain biking. To avoid parking at the scout camp, start at BHNF Road 299.1G, about ¾ mile south of the scout camp. You can ride the ski loop, or try a loop farther north around Odakota Mountain. The north loop combines Trail 23 with BHNF Roads 299, 301, and 693. To climb Odakota Mountain, hike east at a small saddle near the north end of BHNF Road 693. There is a faint blazed trail to the top, but no marker on the flat summit.

The mountain pine beetle has found Bear Mountain to its liking. Pine beetles reach epidemic proportions in the Black Hills about every twenty years attacking crowded stands of ponderosa pines, where trees average 7 to 13 inches in diameter. These pests have destroyed over 5,100 acres of forest between the scout camp and Bear Mountain. Noting that beetle damage ends near open, recently logged stands, the Black Hills National Forest counterattacked by awarding emergency timber contracts. This timber salvage should reduce the spread of the infestation to healthy trees and reduce fuel and fire danger. Ironically, it was the absence of natural fire and the inability of previous logging contractors to thin ponderosa pine stands that contributed to the epidemic. Pines infested with mountain pine beetles remain green in the winter, but can be recognized as they turn yellow in the spring, then red in the summer.

Partly as a result of the timber salvage sale, the Black Hills National Forest plans to rehabilitate much of the Bear Mountain trail system. In 1993 trails will be remarked and inventoried. Relocations, and possibly additions to the trail system, may occur in the future.

For More Information: Contact Harney Ranger District, HCR 87 Box 51, Hill City, SD 57745, (605) 574-2534.

Flume Trail
BLACK HILLS NATIONAL FOREST

▲ **Description:** A hike along an abandoned flume from Spring Creek to Boulder Hill, and a climb to the top of Boulder Hill.
▲ **General Location:** Eight miles northeast of Hill City, South Dakota.
▲ **Access:** To reach the Upper Spring Creek Trailhead, leave U.S. 385 on the Sheridan Lake Road and drive 1.9 miles east before turning south at a sign for the trailhead. Drive 0.4 mile on a dirt road to reach the parking area. To reach the Boulder Hill Trailhead, leave U.S. 16 at 2.5 miles west of Rockerville, and turn right on County Road C233 which is paved for 0.1 mile. Turn left on BHNF Road 358 until reaching the trailhead.
▲ **Distance:** 8 miles one way. Groups with two vehicles can leave one at each trailhead to avoid retracing their route.
▲ **Maps:** Black Hills National Forest Flume Trail Map; USGS Mt. Rushmore, South Dakota, 7.5-minute quadrangle.

One of the most interesting hiking trails in the Black Hills follows the route of a historic flume from Sheridan Lake to the old town of Rockerville. Only the most interesting section, from the Upper Spring Creek Trailhead to Boulder Hill, is described here.

From the Upper Spring Creek Trailhead, the Flume Trail follows a dirt road which winds upstream to the face of the Sheridan Dam. Along the way, it crosses Spring Creek five times, and also passes a point where a torrent of water pours out of a cliff in a scene reminiscent of one of the climatic moments in the movie *Indiana Jones and the Temple of Doom*. Creek crossings may be difficult in spring and early summer due to high water. Most crossings can be made on large rocks placed in the stream, but these do not guarantee dry feet.

Intersect the Centennial Trail just south of the dam. From this intersection the Centennial Trail leads east 1 mile to the Flume (or Calumet) Trailhead or 1.3 miles north to the Dakota Point Trailhead.

From the dam, follow the Flume Trail along the old flume bed to a long tunnel, then a shorter tunnel. Both are interesting breaks from

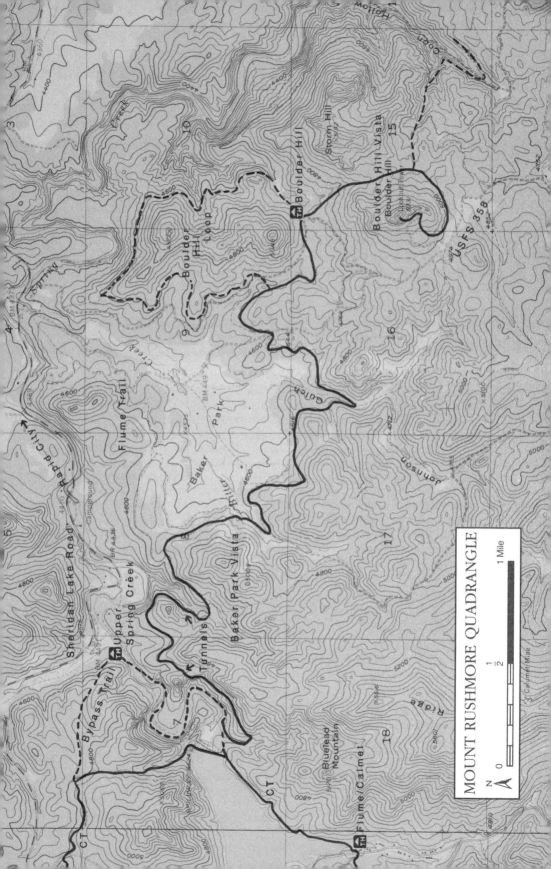

MOUNT RUSHMORE QUADRANGLE

N

0   ½   1 Mile

typical hiking scenery. The tunnels are great places to escape the sun on a hot day, or to take shelter on a rainy day. From the tunnels, continue east to the Baker Park Vista for a view of Boulder Hill.

From the Baker Park Vista, continue east along the flume bed to the start of the Boulder Hill loop. Follow the south part of the loop to the Boulder Hill Trailhead. Continue south on the Flume Trail to a side trail which leads three-quarters mile to the top of Boulder Hill. Boulder Hill offers the best view of the Black Hills from the Flume Trail.

If you arranged a car shuttle simply hike back to the Boulder Hill Trailhead. If you need to return to the Upper Spring Creek Trailhead, take a shortcut which leaves the main Flume Trail from the site of Tunnel Base Camp and leads to Spring Creek. Tunnel Base Camp is located between the two tunnels.

The Black Hills gold rush was booming in 1880 when prospectors discovered placer gold near what was to become the town of Rockerville. Processing of the gold ore was hampered by a lack of water until the Black Hills Placer Mining Company constructed a flume to divert water from Spring Creek, above the old townsite of Sheridan, for use at the Rockerville diggings. Construction of the flume was a massive engineering project which involved the construction of 17.5 miles of canals and troughs, digging of two tunnels, building of a dam near Sheridan and the construction of trestles that were up to eighty feet high. Lack of maintenance on the flume by the late 1880s reduced its flow, and the diggings at Rockerville slowly withered.

The builders of the flume left their legacy to future Black Hills residents in the flume bed which has an overall grade of two percent. From the outlet of Sheridan Lake to Coon Hollow near Rockerville, the Flume Trail generally follows the bed. A few sections are located away from the flume bed to avoid private land or places where trestles bypassed steep gullies. The Flume Trail also includes a loop north of Boulder Hill, and side trails to the top of Boulder Hill and to the Upper Spring Creek Trailhead.

The Flume Trail was designated a national recreation trail in 1979, primarily for its historic significance. In order to preserve the flume bed, it is open to foot travel only. Motorized vehicles, horses, and mountain bikes are not allowed. The trail is an ideal route for a family hike. The terrain is level and it is one of the best marked and maintained trails in the Black Hills National Forest. There are numerous interpretive signs and trail maps located along the way. An unusual feature of the trail is patches of scrub oak amid the pines, spruce, aspen, and birch more typical of the Black Hills.

For More Information: Contact Pactola Ranger District, 803 Soo San Drive, Rapid City, SD 57702, (605) 343-1567.

Deerfield Lake Loop Trail

BLACK HILLS NATIONAL FOREST

▲ **Description:** An easy trail which circles Deerfield Lake.
▲ **General Location:** Sixteen miles northwest of Hill City, South Dakota.
▲ **Access:** From Hill City, drive west on Pennington County Road C308 (BHNF Road 17) 14 miles to BHNF Road 465. Turn north onto Road 465 for 0.1 mile to the Gold Run Trailhead. From Rochford, drive 0.6 miles south on Pennington County Road C306 (BHNF Road 231). Turn left on C306 (BHNF Road 17), and drive 9.2 miles to BHNF Road 417. Turn left onto Road 417 and drive 1.5 miles south to the Custer Trails Campground.
▲ **Distance:** The loop is 11.1 miles around.
▲ **Maps:** Black Hills National Forest Deerfield Lake Loop Trail; USGS Deerfield, South Dakota, 7.5-minute quadrangle.

Completed in 1991, the Deerfield Lake Loop Trail is the newest hiking trail in the Black Hills. The trail is open to horseback riders, hikers, and mountain bikers. So far, horses and bikes appear to be the most popular. Most of the trail follows old two-track dirt roads, but new trail has been constructed from about the North Shore Trailhead to Castle Creek, below the Deerfield Dam. The trail could be good for cross-country skiing, although from Gold Run to the gauging station at the head of Castle Creek it follows the Black Hills Snowmobile Trail 2.

From the Gold Run Trailhead, cross BHNF Road 17 then follow a two-track road to the west. At 0.9 mile cross a gate and gravel BHNF Road 691. Descend to a meadow where a side trail leads north to the Hilltop Trailhead. At 1.3 miles a side road leads south, at 1.6 miles go left at a T-junction. Another side road leads left at 1.8 miles, then the trail descends to reach BHNF Road 17 at 2.4 miles.

Follow BHNF Road 17 and Snowmobile Trail 2 west. Cross a bridge over Castle Creek, then follow a two-track dirt road into an area logged in 1991 and 1992 along the north shore of Deerfield Lake. At 3.2 miles cross a gate then go right at a junction with BHNF Road 461-1F. At 3.4 miles pass a side road left and then go straight through a T-junction onto a foot trail. A side road leads north to the North Shore Trailhead at 3.9 miles.

Continue through timber on the north shore to reach gravel BHNF Road 417 and Custer Trail Trailhead at 5.8 miles. The trail then enters Reynolds Prairie, climbs in and out of numerous gullies and crosses fences at 6.4 and 7.2 miles.

At 7.7 miles descend to a gravel road below the spillway of Deerfield Dam. Continue straight ahead on a dirt road to reach a junction at 8.1 miles with the Deerfield Trail 40, which follows BHNF Road 607-1D.

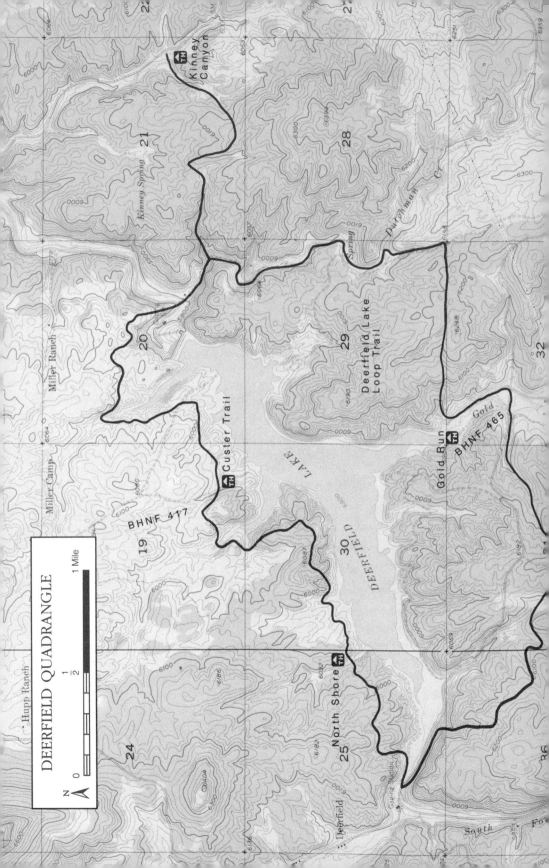

The Deerfield Lake Loop Trail 40L stays right and follows BHNF Road 607-1C. At 8.5 miles a side trail leads west to Dutchman Campground and at 8.8 miles BHNF Road 607-1E leaves to the east.

Climb south alongside gravel BHNF Road 607 past a junction with BHNF Road 607-1A. At 9.7 miles cross Road 607 and turn west onto a ridge in an area logged in 1991. Follow a series of old logging roads on the ridge before descending to Gold Run Gulch at 10.8 miles. Head south along a fence to BHNF Road 17 and the close of the loop at 11.1 miles.

The Deerfield Lake Trail is well marked with brown carsonite posts labeled "L-40" and with gray plastic diamonds. Most of the trailheads have a signboard with a map of the trail on it. Old horse trails which intersect the Deerfield Lake Trail on the east side are marked with carsonite posts with a picture of a horse and gray reflective diamonds. These horse trails can be confused with the main trail. The logging that obliterated part of the trail soon after it was constructed will be complete by 1993, and should not detract from future use of the trail.

Drinking water is available at the many campgrounds and picnic areas around the lake. The best feature of the trail, and an unusual one for the Black Hills, is the proximity to good swimming beaches. A cool swim after a long hike is hard to beat. The trail is ideally situated for use by campers since it passes through or adjacent to Custer trails and Dutchman campgrounds and Gold Run Trailhead. The full loop should take about six hours of hiking, but shorter out-and-back hikes could be made from any of the campgrounds.

The Deerfield Lake loop will eventually be connected to the Centennial Trail by the Deerfield Trail. The Deerfield Trail is complete (1992) east to Pactola Lake, but not all trail marking and bridge construction is finished.

Deerfield Dam was built in 1942 to 1946 by conscientious objectors to World War II. About five hundred men, mostly Mennonites, were assigned to the project by their draft boards because their religious beliefs prohibited them from bearing arms.

For More Information: Contact Harney Ranger District, HCR 87 Box 51, Hill City, SD 57745, (605) 574-2534.

Deerfield Trail and Silver Peak

BLACK HILLS NATIONAL FOREST

▲ **Description:** An easy trip on a railroad grade along Rapid Creek. Silver Mountain is a difficult cross-country scramble.
▲ **General Location:** One mile west of Silver City, South Dakota.

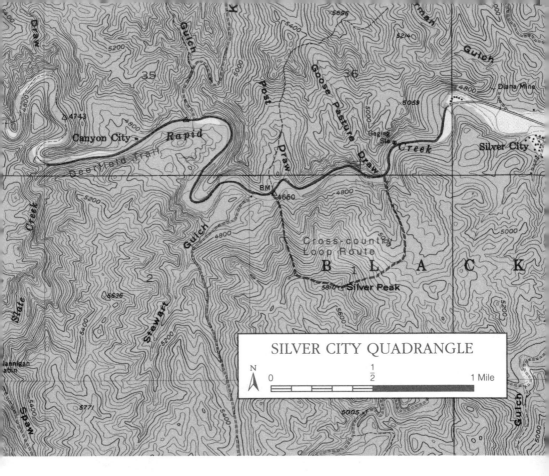

SILVER CITY QUADRANGLE

N

0   ½   1 Mile

▲ **Access:** From U.S. 385 drive 4.6 miles west and south on paved BHNF Road 321 to Silver City. Before crossing Rapid Creek, turn right at a sign for the trailhead onto a gravel road and drive 0.5 mile to a parking area at a locked gate.
▲ **Distance:** It is 3 miles from the parking area to Slate Creek. A climb to the top of Silver Mountain adds 1.5 miles and 1,200 feet of climbing.
▲ **Maps:** Black Hills National Forest; USGS Silver City, South Dakota, 7.5-minute quadrangle.

The Deerfield Trail will eventually connect the Centennial Trail to the Deerfield Lake Loop Trail and will also cross the Black Hills Burlington Northern Heritage Trail. Construction of this connecting trail is incomplete, but for now the Deerfield Trail provides access to one of the prettiest canyons in the Black Hills. The route is designed for hikers, and is closed to motorized vehicles. Mountain biking, horseback riding, and cross-country skiing are also possible. The primary use is for fishing access. The Black Hills National Forest describes the trout fishing as "some of the best and most challenging" in the Black Hills.

This is an ideal trail for a hot summer day. The route follows an old railroad bed on the floor of the canyon. All twelve bridges across the creek have been removed and only at low water and late in summer, can the creek be crossed with dry feet on large boulders. The Black Hills

National Forest plans to build bridges across Rapid Creek. Until then, these crossings are best addressed as opportunities for quick, refreshing swims rather than as obstacles to be overcome. There are a few pools near the crossings to relax in, and the water is warmer than expected.

The Deerfield Trail leaves Rapid Creek and turns south up Slate Creek on a trail completed in 1992. By 1993, the trail is scheduled to be completed and marked all the way to Deerfield Lake. The new route will combine old forest roads, railroad grades, and newly constructed trail. Trailheads are planned for Goose Pasture Draw, Mystic Road, and Kenny Canyon.

Regardless of the season, the canyon is a beautiful walk. It is deep with steep walls and heavily covered in spruce. Mining first brought men to Rapid Creek. They took little ore from the narrow veins, but left small adits and prospect pits scattered throughout the canyon. Many of their cabin sites would make excellent campsites today. Do not disturb any historic sites or relics you encounter.

The north ridges of 5,810-foot Silver Peak are best reached from Rapid Creek between Stewart Gulch and Goose Pasture Draw. There is a large cairn on the summit and a good view to the south of Scruton Mountain and the Seth Bullock Fire Tower. Plan on taking over an hour for this 1,200-foot climb.

For More Information: Contact Pactola Ranger District, 803 Soo San Drive, Rapid City, SD 57702, (605) 343-1567.

Swede Gulch
BLACK HILLS NATIONAL FOREST

▲ **Description:** An easy cross-country ski trip or mountain bike ride through a proposed wilderness area.
▲ **General Location:** Six miles northwest of Rochford, South Dakota.
▲ **Access:** From Rochford, drive 5.1 miles north on the Rochford Road to BHNF Road 259. Drive 0.4 mile south on Road 259, cross Swede Gulch and park at the junction of BHNF Roads 259 and 367. Or, drive south from Lead on U.S. 85, and turn south on the Rochford Road. Then drive 10 miles south to the abandoned town of Nahant, and turn right onto BHNF Road 259.
▲ **Distance:** 6.2-mile round trip and an optional 6-mile extra loop.
▲ **Maps:** Black Hills National Forest Map; USGS Nahant, South Dakota, 7.5-minute quadrangle.

If you're looking for a quiet, easy place to do some off-trail skiing, Swede Gulch is the place for you. This little-used area offers a creekside

Notch Trail, Badlands. Tim Schoon.

Badlands National Park. Tim Schoon.

Sage Creek Area, Badlands Wilderness. Hiram Rogers.

Trail up Bear Butte, Centennial Trail, South Dakota. Edward Raventon.

Cathedral Spires, Black Hills. Edward Raventon.

Aspen Grove, Black Hills. Edward Raventon.

Mountain Goats near Harney Peak, Black Hills. Hiram Rogers.

Cross-country Skier, Eagle Cliff, Black Hills. Hiram Rogers.

Triplet Fawns, Black Hills. Edward Raventon.

Prairie Rattlesnake, Black Hills. Edward Raventon.

Bison, Black Hills. Edward Raventon.

Devils Tower, Wyoming. Tim Schoon.

Belle Fourche River and red beds, near Devils Tower. Tim Schoon.

Painted Canyon, Theodore Roosevelt National Park. Bruce M. Kaye, NPS.

Badlands, Theodore Roosevelt National Park. North Dakota Tourism.

route through some of the prettiest terrain in the central Black Hills. Even when snow conditions are poor elsewhere in the hills, the sheltered canyons of Swede Gulch and Tillson Creek hold their snow against the onslaught of sun and warm temperature.

From the junction of BHNF Roads 259 and 367, ski west for 1.2 miles on BHNF Road 367, which is not maintained in the winter. Beyond the gate at the end of Road 367 snowmobiles and motorized vehicles are prohibited. Ski around the gate, turn south, and enter the narrow canyon of Swede Gulch. From the gate is it 1.9 miles to the confluence of Swede Gulch and Tillson Creek. Along the way you'll pass steep, heavily wooded slopes and dramatic rock walls. You'll see the tracks of deer and wild turkeys and pass a chain of abandoned beaver ponds.

Most skiers will turn around at the junction, but ambitious and strong skiers can make a 6-mile loop from this point. To ski the loop, continue up Swede Gulch crossing through a gate in a fence. At a prominent fork, 1.7 miles past the confluence and just before crossing a creek, turn northwest and follow the fork to Snowmobile Trail 2. Follow Trail 2 north over a saddle, then reach Tillson Creek 2.9 miles past the confluence. At the bottom of the hill turn east off Trail 2 to follow the narrow, overgrown canyon of Tillson Creek. Deep snow and dense timber make this descent difficult, even though it is a gentle downhill grade. Skiers surviving this section will emerge into a meadow just after crossing a fence at 4.3 miles. From the meadow, continue to follow Tillson Creek southeast back to the junction with Swede Gulch for a total distance of 6 miles.

The Black Hills National Forest manages the Swede Gulch area with an emphasis on semi-primitive non-motorized recreation. Hiking, horseback riding, hunting, and cross-country skiing are allowed activities, but no improvements have been made. Despite this management emphasis, Swede Gulch is a place for solitude; the area is seldom travelled.

The long ski loop which connects the upper ends of Swede Gulch and Tillson Creek makes an excellent mountain bike ride in the summer. Riders will probably want to start at the gate across BHNF Road 267 to avoid 1.2 miles of gravel road each way. Livestock graze in Swede Gulch, but roads are closed to the public.

Swede Gulch is part of the 12,000-acre Black Fox Wilderness which has been proposed by the Sierra Club and other conservation organizations. The Black Fox Wilderness will protect the forests of the upper Rapid Creek watershed. Much of the area is old growth and contains diverse age and stand densities of ponderosa pine, white spruce, and quaking aspen. Numerous springs in the area maintain dependable riparian sites.

For More Information: Contact Nemo Ranger District, P.O. Box 407, Deadwood, SD 57732, (605) 578-2744; or Two Wheeler Dealer, 310 W. Jackson Blvd., Spearfish, SD 57783, (605) 642-7545.

Custer Peak
BLACK HILLS NATIONAL FOREST

▲ **Description:** A difficult cross-country ski trip or a long, moderate mountain bike trip.

▲ **General Location:** Seven miles south of Lead, South Dakota.

▲ **Access:** From U.S. 85 at Brownsville turn west onto the Englewood Road (BHNF Road 227). Drive 2.1 miles west then turn south onto BHNF Road 229. Drive 1.4 miles to the end of the plowed road and park. To approach the peak from the west via Snowmobile Trail 7, drive 7.2 miles south of Lead on the Rochford Road and park at the Dumont Lot. To approach from the east, drive south of Brownsville on U.S. 385 for 1.8 miles. Turn west onto BHNF Road 216 and drive a short distance to the Custer Lot which is opposite a large gravel pit.

▲ **Distance:** From the north it is 2.7 miles one way to the summit. From the west it is 5.3 miles one way to the summit. The two routes on the east side can be combined to form a 10-mile loop.

▲ **Maps:** Black Hills National Forest; USGS Deadwood South, Lead, Minnesota Ridge, and Nahant, South Dakota, 7.5-minute quadrangles.

A cross-country ski trip to the top of Custer Peak is a challenging and rewarding climb to one of the most scenic vistas in the northern Black Hills. The flat cone of Custer Peak is one of the most recognizable landmarks in the Black Hills, and a climb to the top can be made in any season.

The north approach begins by following an unmarked extension of BHNF Road 229 south along Elk Creek. Continue south on a lesser fork where the main fork turns west. At the end of the meadows along the headwaters of Elk Creek, turn left again at another stream junction and begin to climb steadily. At 1.3 miles reach a prominent saddle on the west shoulder of Custer Peak.

At the saddle turn left and north onto Snowmobile Trail 7 and follow the trail for 0.1 mile. Then turn right and east and follow an obvious dirt road which spirals up the summit cone of Custer Peak to end just short of the lookout tower on the summit. The original wood lookout tower on the summit was built in 1911.

The tower is an excellent spot to rest, eat lunch, and enjoy the views. Bear Butte, Harney Peak, Deer Mountain, and Terry Peak are particularly prominent. To return, follow your tracks back to Elk Creek. The

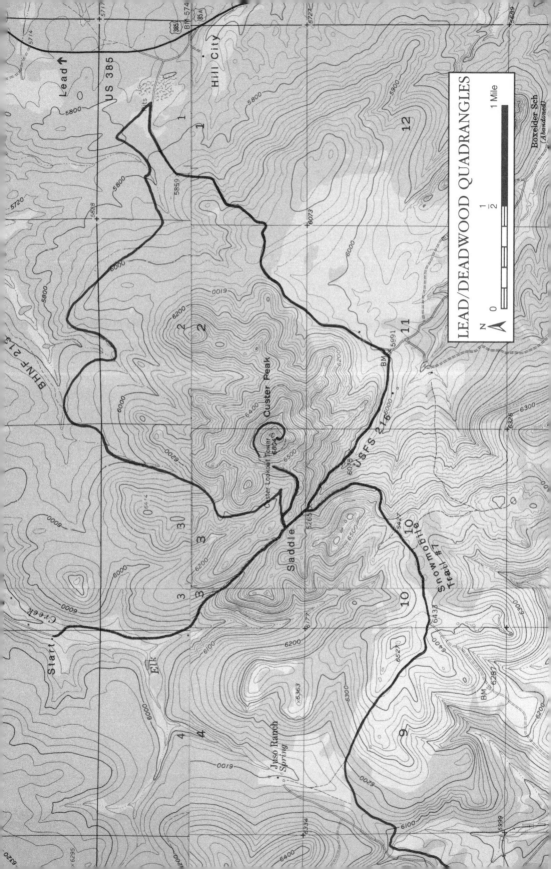

LEAD/DEADWOOD QUADRANGLES

N

0   ½   1 Mile

Lead ↑

US 385

BHNF 213

Hill City

Custer Peak

Custer Lookout Towers

USFS 216

Saddle

Elk

Snowmobile Trail #7

Start

Creek

Jyso Ranch Spring

Boxelder Sch (Abandoned)

BM 5991

BM 6287

steep, narrow trail from the meadows on Elk Creek to the shoulder of Custer Peak can be very difficult to descend, especially on icy snow.

Snowmobile Trail 7 leads to Custer Peak from the Rochford Road on the west side. The route follows a route toward Juso Ranch before climbing east just below ridge 6,527. Trail 7 then leads northeast to point 6,427 before turning north to reach the west saddle.

A loop on the east side of Custer Peak combines Snowmobile Trail 7 with BHNF Road 216. Road 216 is plowed in the winter, so this loop is best done as a summer mountain bike ride. From the Custer Lot follow Road 216 west 3.3 miles to the west shoulder, then to the summit. Return to the west shoulder and follow Trail 7 east.

Trail 7 winds down the north slope of Custer Peak to a fork 1.3 miles from the shoulder. Old Snowmobile Trail 5 used to follow BHNF Road 213 down the left fork, but Road 213 is now blocked by private land. Snowmobile Trail 7 follows the right fork along BHNF Road 213 southeast for 1.9 miles. Just before Road 213 crosses a fork of Bear Butte Creek and reaches Road 216, turn left (east) onto a rough dirt road. Follow the dirt road for 0.5 mile and turn right off the road just before reaching a gate. The right fork leads 0.3 mile to the Custer Lot.

A major timber sale is planned for the east side of Custer Peak around Snowmobile Trail 7 and BHNF Road 213. Expect the roads in this area to change considerably in the future.

Custer's 1874 expedition to the Black Hills named the peak for its leader. Surprisingly the group made no attempt to scale the peak. The Custer Peak Lookout Tower is staffed throughout the summer.

For More Information: Contact Nemo Ranger District, P.O. Box 407, Deadwood, SD 57732, (605) 578-2744; or Two Wheeler Dealer 310 W. Jackson Blvd., Spearfish, SD 57783, (605) 642-7545.

Lander–Yellow Jacket Loop
BLACK HILLS NATIONAL FOREST

▲ **Description:** An easy cross-country ski or mountain bike loop on Black Hills National Forest roads.
▲ **General Location:** Fifteen miles southwest of Lead, South Dakota.
▲ **Distance:** 6.9 miles for the ski loop and 8.4 miles for the mountain bike loop.
▲ **Access:** From Cheyenne Crossing, drive southwest 6.7 miles on U.S. 85 to BHNF Road 232 and leave one car here. Drive another 0.8 mile and park the other car at the Eagle Cliff–Bratwurst Trailhead. The route begins across the highway from the trailhead.
▲ **Maps:** Black Hills National Forest; USGS Crook's Tower, South Dakota, 7.5-minute quadrangle.

CROOKS TOWER QUADRANGLE

The Lander–Yellow Jacket loop is an easy family ski tour or mountain bike ride through the area south of the Eagle Cliff cross-country ski trail system. This is an area heavily used by local skiers who also call it "Clayton Draw" or "Half-Painted Corral." Lander–Yellow Jacket forms the western edge of a new system of cross-country ski trails around North Park and Ward Draw which are being developed by local skiers.

From the Eagle Cliff–Bratwurst parking lot, cross U.S. 85 and ski south along a road through an open meadow. This part of the loop is on private property. An unmarked cross-country ski route, called the "Aspen Grove," can be used to bypass the private land on the east side. Stay in the main draw for 2.5 miles, passing Lander Spring, before cresting a small divide in a grove of spruce. After another 0.3 mile, turn left (east) at an old corral into a narrow side draw which leads to BHNF Road 232 and the valley of Spearfish Creek. This side canyon contains a few short, narrow drops with easy run-outs that are great fun. If you miss the side canyon you will intersect Snowmobile Trail 2 and BHNF Road 231 in 0.4 mile.

Follow BHNF Road 232 north along Spearfish Creek back to U.S. 85. Upper Spearfish Canyon is not as steep or dramatic as the lower canyon, but is nearly as beautiful. Pass a junction with BHNF Road 210 after 2.8 miles. The last 0.7 mile is icier and has less snow than the rest of the route. If your group has only one vehicle, you will need to turn left and ski west along the road back to the trailhead.

Several factors combine to make this an excellent family trip. The terrain is gentle and there are no steep hills. The loop is uphill going out and downhill on the way back. If the loop is done counterclockwise, it is mostly downhill. Route finding is easy and much of the route may be packed by snowmobiles. Groups not wishing to ski the entire loop may simply ski up and down either one of the draws.

This loop is in the "buffer zone" between cross-country ski and snowmobile areas and is used by both groups. Some novice skiers may appreciate the tracks left by snowmobilers, while fitness-oriented skiers can often skate across the packed areas.

Lander Draw holds snow well into April and may have the best spring skiing in the Black Hills. Skaters in particular will relish blasting across the hard, fast crust which is heaven when covered by a dusting of fresh powder from a late spring storm.

With the arrival of summer, and dry ground, this is a good mountain bike loop. To keep on two-track dirt roads, continue south on BHNF Road 231.5B, avoiding the side draw, to reach BHNF Road 231 at 0.4 mile past the corral. Turn east and follow Road 231 for 0.5 mile, then turn south on BHNF Road 232. Ride 0.4 mile to return to ski route. Most bikers won't mind the 0.8-mile trip along the highway to close the loop, so two vehicles are not needed. Avoid this loop in wet conditions because of sticky, clay-rich soils on the limestone bedrock. While this is a relatively easy ride by bike, keep in mind that only Roads 231 and 232 are maintained and riding elsewhere can be rough.

For More Information: Contact Spearfish Ranger District, 2014 N. Main St., Spearfish, SD 57783, (605) 642-4622.

Ward Draw
BLACK HILLS NATIONAL FOREST

▲ **Description:** A long loop over moderate terrain suitable for skiers and mountain bikers.
▲ **General Location:** Ten miles south of Lead, South Dakota.
▲ **Access:** From the junction of U.S. 85 and the Rochford Road, drive 2.5 south miles to a sign for the Lead Country Club. Turn right onto the Hanna Road which becomes BHNF Road 196, then drive 2.4 miles to the junction with BHNF Road 209. Park here, or in a small parking area which is on the west side of the road 0.1 mile south.
▲ **Distance:** The loop is 9.4 miles around.
▲ **Maps:** Black Hills National Forest; USGS Lead, Savoy, Crook's Tower, and Nahant, South Dakota, 7.5-minute quadrangles.

Ward Draw, and the area surrounding Hanna, are among the coldest areas in the Black Hills. This is a place to be if you are looking for good late-season snow, and for excellent cross-country ski terrain.

From the junction of BHNF Roads 196 and 209, ski south on Road 209 for 0.8 mile along Ward Draw to a junction with BHNF Road 212. Stay left on Road 212, and continue to follow Ward Draw which enters a steep, narrow canyon. The sides of the draw are covered in spruce and ponderosa pine. This part of Ward Draw is similar to Dead Ox Gulch in the Eagle Cliff Ski Area.

Continue up Ward Draw for 1.1 mile, past a building used by the City of Lead Water Department. In upper Ward Draw, the canyon becomes even steeper and narrower. Once in the upper draw skiers have several options. The simplest is to continue to follow the main draw until it merges with BHNF Road 206-2L near Harvey Spring 1.8 miles from the cabin. An alternate route leaves the main draw 0.6 mile beyond the water building, and leads directly to Well Park.

BHNF Road 206-2L quickly leads to a major road. Turn right and follow this road past Well Park to a four-way junction with BHNF Road 209

CROOKS TOWER/NAHANT

which is 1.8 miles from Road 206-2L. This intersection is the highest elevation on the loop, and a good spot to stop for lunch after nearly six miles of gradual uphill. Turn right at the intersection onto BHNF Road 209 and enjoy a fast, well-deserved descent into the bottom of Long Draw. Follow Long Draw past the Ward Cemetery and Graveyard Spring back to the junction of Roads 209 and 212. From this junction, retrace your route on Road 209 back to the Hanna Road.

Mountain bikers will find the Ward Draw loop varied and challenging. To avoid repeating the start of the loop, bikers can park at the junction of BHNF Roads 209 and 212. Beyond the Lead Water Supply Building, Ward Draw can be a difficult slog on cattle trails. Once into the headwaters, in Section 15, many riders will be forced to dismount and push their bikes. But, there is plenty of easy downhill riding on gravel BHNF Road 209.

Although Ward Draw loop is long, all the climbing comes at the beginning, so skiers have a reasonably easy return route. Route finding is easy. The only complicated area is at the head of Ward Draw, and if you do get confused here any side draw will lead eventually to the road which connects Harvey Spring to Well Park on the way to BHNF Road 209.

The scenery is fabulous. Ward Draw is the prettiest of the many north-south trending canyons located south of U.S. 85. This is a cold, snowy place which offers good skiing even when other trails have spring conditions at best. The south part of the area is close to Snowmobile Trail 2, so snow machines may be found along the route from Harvey Spring to Hanna via BHNF Road 209. Ward Draw is not passable by snowmobile.

For More Information: Contact Spearfish Ranger District, 2014 N. Main St., Spearfish, SD 57783, (605) 642-4622.

Holey Rock–Clifftop Trails Loop
Eagle Cliff Trails
BLACK HILLS NATIONAL FOREST

▲ **Description:** A moderate mountain bike or cross-country ski loop through the heart of the Eagle Cliff trails.
▲ **General Location:** Fifteen miles southwest of Lead, South Dakota.
▲ **Access:** From Cheyenne Crossing, drive southwest 8.4 miles on U.S. 85 to the Eagle Cliff Trailhead. Park in the lot located on the north side of the highway. This lot is plowed in winter by the South Dakota Department of Transportation.

▲ **Distance:** A 6.1-mile loop with many optional side trips.
▲ **Maps:** Black Hills National Forest Eagle Cliff Trails Map; USGS Crook's Tower and Savoy, South Dakota, 7.5-minute quadrangles.

The arrival of summer at Eagle Cliff used to signal a respite for the trails from their avalanche of winter visitors. However, the Black Hills National Forest now keeps the trails open for summer use by hikers, mountain bikers, and horseback riders. Mountain biking is by far the most popular use, and once the trails have dried out in early summer, the tracks of fat tires replace those of skinny skis.

A loop from the Holey Rock–Lily Park Trailhead to Clifftop best illustrates the potential fun of mountain biking or hiking at Eagle Cliff. The starts of both the Holey Rock and Lily Park trails are narrow, steep, and winding. Beginning skiers struggle on these sections of trail, which are the most difficult at Eagle Cliff, but the trails are navigable by novice hikers and bikers.

To follow the loop counterclockwise, begin on the Lily Park Trail. Cross a fence through a gate and follow Lily Park for 0.5 mile to the Bratwurst Trail, which is also BHNF Road 179. Turn east on Bratwurst and go 0.4 mile to Wipe Out which is BHNF Road 179.1B. Not surprisingly, Wipe Out is a steep descent which leads to Intake Meadows after 0.4 mile. Follow Intake Meadows for 0.8 mile passing through a gate in a fence just past the junction with Lost Run. Turn east onto Eagle Cliff and head 0.3 mile to the east end of the Clifftop Trail.

The gentle grades of Intake Meadows and Eagle Cliff become just fond memories as the climb to Clifftop begins. After a level section on Clifftop, the descent back to the Eagle Cliff Trail is just as steep, so be careful to control your speed over the many berms on the trail in this narrow canyon. Once back on the Eagle Cliff Trail go west, then south for 0.2 mile to a gate and the start of the Hidden Basin Trail.

Hidden Basin climbs steadily over a small knob, then descends gradually to reach Bratwurst after 0.8 mile. Turn west on Bratwurst and go 0.3 mile to the Holey Rock Trail. A gate across the Holey Rock Trail marks the beginning of a difficult descent along switchbacks to the trailhead which is 0.9 mile from Bratwurst.

This basic route has many simple variations. For a longer trip, use Lost Run or Deep Snow between Bratwurst and Intake Meadows. To shorten the loop from the east end of Intake Meadows, head directly west on Eagle Cliff all the way to Hidden Basin, instead of using the Clifftop Trail.

The Black Hills National Forest has worked hard at opening Eagle Cliff for year-round recreation. The trails are well blazed, easy to follow,

and almost every intersection is marked by a sign. Maps of the trail system are generally available near the trailheads. With the exception of Bratwurst, which is a well-used road, the other trails on this loop are two-track dirt roads well suited to mountain bikes.

Eagle Cliff is a multiple-use area. Cattle graze in the area and could be a hazard to bikers. Eagle Cliff is part of the Limestone Diversity Unit for which the Black Hills National Forest has planned a controversial timber sale.

For More Information: Contact Spearfish Ranger District, 2014 N. Main, Spearfish, SD 57783, (605) 642-4622, or stop by the Cheyenne Crossing Store.

Dead Ox–Roller Coaster Trails Loop
Eagle Cliff Trails
BLACK HILLS NATIONAL FOREST

▲ **Description:** A moderate cross-country ski tour or mountain bike ride in the north side of the Eagle Cliff trails.
▲ **General Location:** Thirteen miles southwest of Lead, South Dakota.
▲ **Access:** From the junction of U.S. 14A and 85 at Cheyenne Crossing, drive 4 miles southwest on U.S. 85 to a Black Hills National Forest picnic area on the southeast side of the road. The Dead Ox Trail starts directly across the highway in the yard of a summer home. In the winter this trailhead is maintained by the Northern Hills Cross-country Ski Club and Black Hills National Forest, which has an easement through the cabin property. Mountain bike riders who wish to ride the loop in the summer can start from the unmarked Raddick Trailhead located 0.7 mile further down U.S. 85 on the north side of the road.
▲ **Distance:** The ski loop is 7.1 miles long and the mountain bike loop is 6.5 miles long.
▲ **Maps:** Black Hills National Forest Eagle Cliff Trails; USGS Savoy, South Dakota, 7.5-minute quadrangle.

The Dead Ox–Roller Coaster loop may be the best ski loop on marked trails in the Black Hills region. It has all the features required for a good tour. The snow is deep and dependable, and is well shaded in Dead Ox and Raddick gulches. The loop is uphill on the way out and downhill on the return, so there is no long grind to finish your tour. Both trails are rolling with some tight downhill turns that should be challenging, but not impossible for most skiers.

From the cabin ski up the valley of Dead Ox Creek 1.1 miles to a gate and the junction with the Rolling Ox Trail. The tight, winding canyon in lower Dead Ox may be the prettiest part of Eagle Cliff. Steep limestone walls are covered with dense coats of spruce and ponderosa pine. Further up the canyon, forested areas mingle with open meadows. Continue up the canyon 1.5 miles to a fork in Dead Ox Creek, a point where snowmobiles illegally penetrate the Eagle Cliff trails. Take the left fork to where the trail turns south near an old stock tank onto an abandoned logging road. After another obscure left turn, the trail crosses Boland Ridge and reaches a junction with the Roller Coaster and What-the-Hell trails 1.1 miles from the fork. Both these turns are easy to miss, but are marked with arrows on wood signs.

The reward for all this climbing is a rollicking descent down the aptly named Roller Coaster. After 1.5 miles of well-deserved downhill skiing, turn left at the junction with the Raddick Gulch Trail, then climb a small ridge. Descend a short distance to the junction with the Rolling Ox Trail 0.6 mile from the junction. The toughest 0.2 mile of the entire loop lies just ahead. Rolling Ox is a steep, narrow descent down a heavily wooded slope which leaves little room for error. Two switchbacks make the descent to Dead Ox Gulch a little easier. From Dead Ox the trail leads a gradual mile downhill back to U.S. 85.

Experienced Black Hills skiers learn to start their trips early in the morning. Afternoon temperatures, particularly in mid to late winter, often climb above freezing. As temperatures climb the top of the snowpack begins to melt producing perfect "snowball" snow which clings to the bottom of skis nullifying any glide. After a mile or so of walking on skis caked with six inches of wet snow some skiers have been known to sleep away the rest of the afternoon and resuming their tours only after the snow has refrozen.

Of course, starting early means that your party is more likely to have to break trail, but remember that part of the fun of cross-country skiing is the exercise and that breaking trail is far easier than skiing through snowball snow.

The Black Hills National Forest does not sanction either the Dead Ox or Raddick trailheads, both of which are on private land. Summer trail users should use Raddick or another trailhead in place of Dead Ox, since the cabin at the head of the gulch is generally occupied in the summer.

Mountain bikers can access the loop via Raddick Gulch. From the Raddick Trailhead, ride 0.4 mile up the gulch to a fence and the start of the Roller Coaster Trail. Ride up the northwest fork of Raddick Gulch on Roller Coaster to the junction with Rolling Ox. Ride down the Rolling Ox Trail into the valley of Dead Ox Creek to a junction with the Dead Ox Trail.

To return to Raddick, exit Roller Coaster onto the Raddick Gulch Trail. Follow the Raddick Gulch Trail 0.9 mile to the gate at the end of

Roller Coaster. Then ride 0.4 mile back down the gulch to U.S. 85. Both Roller Coaster and Raddick Gulch are two-track dirt roads that are fun riding. Dead Ox, however, is simply a cattle track. The northwest fork of Dead Ox (1.1 miles from the four-way junction or 1.5 miles from the Rolling Ox junction) is a two-track dirt road. BHNF Road 733.1A is a two-track gravel road which runs along the top of Boland Ridge.

The 1992 Eagle Cliff Trail Map shows the result of the Forest Service's efforts to reduce "trail density" at Eagle Cliff. Trail names are consolidated on the new map and a few trails, many of them short spur trails, are no longer on the map. These old trails still can be skied, they just will not be maintained, marked, or shown on the map. If you can't find a 1990-91 edition of the map (they are printed on green paper) try following stray tracks, open slopes through the woods, or just your own intuition to find new trails.

Trail ratings at Eagle Cliff are conservative and are based in part on trail length. Although rated most difficult, the terrain along Dead Ox is moderate and suitable for intermediate or strong beginner skiers, although almost anyone can face plant on this trail if their attention wavers at the wrong moment.

For More Information: Contact Spearfish Ranger District, 2014 N. Main, Spearfish, SD 57783, (605) 642-4622, or stop by the Cheyenne Crossing Store.

Sunny Meadow Trails Loop
Eagle Cliff Trails
BLACK HILLS NATIONAL FOREST

▲ **Description:** An easy cross-country ski or mountain bike loop.
▲ **General Location:** Seventeen miles southwest of Lead, South Dakota.
▲ **Access:** From Cheyenne Crossing, drive 9.4 miles southwest on U.S. 85. Park on the north side of the highway at the entrance to Sunny Meadow. The lot is plowed in winter by the Black Hills National Forest and Northern Hills Cross-country Ski Club.
▲ **Distance:** The short loop is 4.2 miles around. A longer loop which adds the Toni's and What-the-Hell trails is 6.6 miles around.
▲ **Maps:** Black Hills National Forest Eagle Cliff Trails; USGS Crook's Tower and Savoy, South Dakota, 7.5-minute quadrangles.

Some of the easiest terrain at Eagle Cliff is on the west side of the area. The small parking area on U.S. 85 allows access to a variety of loop trips perfect for those looking for a gentle tour of the high country.

To ski the short loop counterclockwise, take your first right onto the Bratwurst Trail after crossing the cattleguard. Climb gently to the east on Bratwurst for 1.3 miles to the Hidden Basin Trail. Follow Hidden Basin for 0.8 mile north over a small knob, and then descend a moderately steep grade to rejoin the Sunny Meadow Trail. Return to the trailhead by skiing 2 miles west, then south, on Sunny Meadow.

If you desire a longer route, follow the Hidden Basin Trail to the junction with Toni's Trail. Toni's leads 1.2 miles north up a small draw to a four-way intersection. At the intersection, turn left onto the What-the-Hell Trail and follow it for 1.8 miles west, then south to a junction with the Sunny Meadow Trail. From this junction it is 1.4 miles south on Sunny Meadow back to the trailhead.

These two loops are equally attractive as mountain bike rides in the summer or fall. The What-the-Hell Trail is on rough, two-track dirt roads and trails, but the rest of the trails follow easy two-track roads. Cattle graze at Eagle Cliff in the summer, and seem to particularly favor the north end of the Sunny Meadow Trail. Remember that the soil developed on the Paha Sapa limestone is very slick when wet, so avoid this trail in the spring, and any time after a rain. The trailhead and most of the first 1.5 miles of the Sunny Meadow Trail are on private land. So be careful to respect private property rights as you ride or ski through the area.

Sunny Meadow could just as well been named "Windy Meadow." Without the pervasive tree cover found elsewhere at Eagle Cliff, the wind can howl across the meadow. A windshell and sunscreen are handy to have while skiing here.

For More Information: Contact Spearfish Ranger District, 2014 N. Main, Spearfish, SD 57783, (605) 642-4622, or stop by the Cheyenne Crossing Store.

Little Spearfish Trail
BLACK HILLS NATIONAL FOREST

▲ **Description:** An easy loop trail along Little Spearfish Creek and Ranger Draw for hikers, mountain bikers, horse riders, and cross-country skiers.

▲ **General Location:** Twelve miles west of Lead, South Dakota.

▲ **Access:** From Cheyenne Crossing drive 5.5 miles south on U.S. 14A. Turn left onto BHNF Road 222 and drive 4.8 miles to the trailhead which is located just beyond Timon Campground.

▲ **Distance:** The loop is 5.9 miles around.

▲ **Maps:** Black Hills National Forest Little Spearfish and Rimrock Trail Map; USGS Savoy, South Dakota, 7.5-minute quadrangle.

OLD BALDY MTN./SAVOY

Little Spearfish is the south loop of a trail system near Timon Campground on the Limestone Plateau. This loop is one of the best during the fall color season.

From the trailhead at Timon Campground, the trail leads gradually up the valley of Little Spearfish Creek. After 0.9 mile, the trail crosses the creek on a bridge which is within sight of BHNF Road 134, then begins to climb to the ridge which divides Little Spearfish Creek from Ranger Draw. This climb starts steeply, then becomes more gentle closer to the divide. On the divide reach a dirt road which is adjacent to a fence at 2.5 miles. Follow the dirt road for 0.2 mile where the trail turns north and enters Ranger Draw. A fast descent along Ranger Draw is the well-deserved reward for the climb to the divide.

Ranger Draw joins Little Spearfish Creek and BHNF Road 222 after 4.6 miles and the trail turns to the west. Skiers can follow the trail for 1.3 miles back to Timon Campground, or simply ski back on the road keeping a look out for snowmobiles.

The terrain along this route is difficult for beginning skiers. The route may be too long for children or novice skiers, especially if they have to break trail. The trail is well marked and easy to follow, even when snow covered. Experienced skiers will have no problems, and may want to explore some of the other forest roads that the trail intersects. Snow conditions should be similar to the Eagle Cliff area since the terrain and elevation are similar.

Little Spearfish is one of the best cross-country ski trails in the Black Hills. But all good things have a catch, and for this trail the catch is winter access. BHNF Road 222, which reaches Timon Campground from the east, is part of Snowmobile Trail 4A, and is closed to wheeled vehicles beyond Roughlock Falls after December 1, when maintenance begins on the state snowmobile trail system. BHNF Road 134, which provides access from the west, is not plowed between the 134-222 junction and the 134-733 junction to the south. Access will change every winter based on logging needs and the decision of the county commissioners, so it is best to check beforehand for information. Skiers determined to try the Little Spearfish Trail can either ski up the road from Roughlock Falls, ski south from the BHNF Road 134-222 junction, or ski in from the north along Road 134.

Mountain bikers will find the Little Spearfish Trail ideal. The entire trail is single track, most of it is relatively smooth. Bikers looking for a longer trip can combine the Little Spearfish Trail with one, or both loops of the adjacent Rimrock Trail, which is located north of BHNF Road 222. In early fall, with the aspen covered in bright gold, the trail is a little bit of heaven.

For More Information: Contact Spearfish Ranger District, 2014 N. Main St., Spearfish, SD 57783, (605) 642-4622.

OLD BALDY MTN./SAVOY

Old Baldy Trail

BLACK HILLS NATIONAL FOREST

▲ **Description:** A moderate loop hike, bike, or horse ride to the top of Old Baldy Mountain.

▲ **General Location:** Fifteen miles southwest of Spearfish, South Dakota.

▲ **Access:** From U.S. 14A at Savoy leave Spearfish Canyon on BHNF Road 222. After 6 miles, turn north on BHNF Road 134. Follow Road 134 for 1.2 miles to an unmarked parking area on the west side of the road. The trailhead can also be reached by driving south from Spearfish on BHNF Road 134 for 15.6 miles.

▲ **Distance:** 6.9 miles, including the spur trail to the summit.

▲ **Maps:** Black Hills National Forest; USGS Savoy, South Dakota, and Old Baldy Mtn., Wyoming-South Dakota, 7.5-minute quadrangles.

The newest trail in the Spearfish District of the Black Hills National Forest offers a scenic tour of the northern end of the Limestone Plateau. Built for hikers, horseback riders, mountain bikers, and cross-country skiers, the Old Baldy Trail consists of a loop trail south of Old Baldy Mountain and a side trail to the summit.

The loop begins 150 yards from the trailhead. The west loop follows a ridge west, then north before dropping into the valley of a tributary of Beaver Creek. After descending along the tributary, the trails turns northeast and follows a fence which is the property boundary of Lap Circle Ranch. Beyond the ranch boundary is a rolling section of trail. Just after crossing Snowmobile Trail 3 (this saddle is on the ridge which divides the drainages of Beaver and Iron creeks) the west loop intersects the east loop and the summit spur trail in a meadow 3.3 miles from the trailhead. The loop is essentially a walk through the woods with occasional views of Old Baldy Mountain.

The summit spur follows the divide west then finishes with a steep climb up the cone of Old Baldy Mountain. From the intersection, the east loop leads 0.3 mile to Baldy Lake, a glorified stock pond in an over-grazed meadow. The trail turns south and leads 2.2 miles back to the trailhead on overgrown jeep roads and single track.

The top of Old Baldy offers a few surprises, the first is a scattered covering of ponderosa pines and burr oak, illustrating the power of revegetation on the Limestone Plateau. The best surprise is the view east over Spearfish Canyon to Terry Peak, Ragged Top, and Spearfish Peak. Crow Peak to the north, and the Cement Ridge Lookout, only three miles west, are visible. Open-pit gold mines at Richmond Hill and Annie Creek–Foley Ridge lie on the north and west sides of Terry Peak.

The east loop is underlain primarily by rocks of the Mississippian Age Paha Sapa limestone while the west loop is underlain mostly by Tertiary Age intrusive igneous rocks. Old Baldy is one of the many prominent summits in the northern Black Hills formed from these hard, resistant, intrusive rocks.

The rolling terrain along the loop would be ideal for cross-country skiing. Unfortunately, in some winters there is no maintained access to the trailhead, so call ahead before making the trip. Mountain bikes are popular, though some trail sections can be very rutted and rough for inexperienced bikers. Deer and wild turkeys are common along the trail.

While the loop trail alone is an easy hike, the extra distance and elevation gain of a summit trip make this hike moderately difficult. The full loop with a trip to the summit should take three to four hours. No water or other facilities are available along the trail or at the trailhead. Cattle graze in the area so bring your own water. The trail is in excellent condition, and is well marked with posts and blazes.

For More Information: Contact Spearfish Ranger District, 2014 N. Main, Spearfish, SD 57783, (605) 642-4622.

Red Lake
BLACK HILLS NATIONAL FOREST

▲ **Description:** A moderately difficult cross-country ski or mountain bike trip over unmarked trails.
▲ **General Location:** Ten miles west of Lead, South Dakota.
▲ **Access:** From Spearfish, follow the Iron Creek Road (BHNF Road 134) to the south. After 7 miles, pass the Big Hills Cross-country Ski Area, and after 11.2 miles pass the side road to Iron Creek Lake. Red Lake is 2 miles past the Iron Creek Lake Road. The trailhead is unmarked and you must park on the roadside.
▲ **Distance:** There are 6.1 miles of trails for cross-country skiing.
▲ **Maps:** Black Hills National Forest; USGS Savoy, South Dakota, 7.5-minute quadrangle.

The Red Lake Cross-country Ski Area has been developed by outdoor education majors of Black Hills State University under the supervision of Everett Follette. The trails are designed as an alternative to the Big Hill trails for winters when Big Hill has insufficient snow for ski touring. Red Lake is higher in elevation than Big Hill, so it receives more snow and holds it longer.

There are three main loops at Red Lake. The short loop is located just east of Red Lake, and the long loop extends farther east. An optional route which follows BHNF roads is located south of the other two loops. All three loops start from the same main feeder trail, and all are best skied clockwise.

MAURICE/SAVOY QUADRANGLES

N

0   ½   1 Mile

The Red Lake trails start downhill and east of BHNF Road 134, just across Snowmobile Trail 1. Follow a forest road over a ridge, then across a small draw for 0.6 mile. The first road junction to the south is BHNF Road 225-1A and the end of the optional loop. The next junction in 0.3 mile is the start of the short loop.

Turn left onto the short loop and pass the stockpond that is Red Lake. After 0.2 mile turn right into a gentle draw. A 0.4-mile downhill stretch connects the short loop to the long loop. To complete the short loop, turn right onto BHNF 225-1D and ski back up the draw for 0.5 mile.

To follow the long loop from the junction with BHNF Road 225-1D, ski northeast into a large meadow for 1.2 miles. Start back up the meadow, then climb the hillside to the south for 0.2 mile. This turn can be very difficult to find without ski tracks on it. The grade is steep at first, but soon becomes more gentle as the trail follows a broad ridge. At the top of the loop, a break in the trees offers a view over Little Spearfish Creek. Just before reaching BHNF Road 225-1C, a faint path leads north off of the ridge. Follow the path for 0.4 mile down a steep descent to the head of the large meadow. To close the long loop, continue east down the meadow to a point just east of the junction of the long and short loops.

To follow the optional loop, continue southwest on the ridge past BHNF Road 225-1C. In 0.6 mile, turn north onto BHNF Road 225-1A. Follow 1A for 0.6 mile to the junction located west of Red Lake.

The Red Lake trails cover excellent ski terrain and should have enough snow when snow has melted off other ski trails. None of the hills are especially long or difficult. There is a good mix of hills and flatter sections.

Red Lake is also an interesting area for a summer mountain bike ride. Without ski tracks to follow, the turns both on and off the ridge which forms the south side of the long loop are tough to find. Otherwise most of trails follow two-track dirt roads. Mountain bikers can connect to routes at Iron Creek (described below) or with the BHNF Rimrock Trail.

For More Information: Contact Spearfish Ranger District, 2014 N. Main St., Spearfish, SD 57783, (605) 642-4622; or Ski Cross Country, 701 3rd St., Spearfish, SD 57783, (605) 642-3851.

Iron Creek
BLACK HILLS NATIONAL FOREST

▲ **Description:** An easy and popular hike leading from Spearfish Canyon to the Limestone Plateau.
▲ **General Location:** Eleven miles south of Spearfish, South Dakota.
▲ **Access:** From Cheyenne Crossing, drive 7.2 miles north on U.S. 14A to Iron

Creek or drive 12 miles south down the canyon from Spearfish. A small parking area is located on the west side of the road.

▲ **Distance:** 1.3 miles one way. An additional 0.6-mile route leads north to connect to the Big Hill trails and an additional 1.9-mile route leads south to connect to the unmarked Red Lake Cross-country Ski Area.

▲ **Maps:** Black Hills National Forest; USGS Maurice and Savoy, South Dakota, 7.5-minute quadrangles.

In the dry climate of the Black Hills it is easy to underestimate the power of floods in shaping the landscape. What rain that does fall offers clear evidence of the power of storms. The Black Hills are rarely soaked by long gentle rains. Instead, rain comes hard and quickly as afternoon thunderstorms in the summer, or powerful storms such as the one that flooded Rapid City in 1972.

A good road used to lead from Iron Creek Lake, high on the Limestone Plateau, to Savoy at the bottom of Spearfish Canyon. This road was destroyed by the 1972 flood and abandoned soon after. The route has since overgrown and eroded to the point that only a rough foot trail remains. Because this path is the only easy way to climb out of lower Spearfish Canyon on foot or by mountain bike, it has become one of the more popular hikes in the Black Hills.

From the parking area at U.S. 14A in Spearfish Canyon, cross through a rock barricade and head west up Iron Creek. The route is unmarked, but the trail is obvious. The old road is rocky and eroded, but still easy walking. After 1.3 miles reach another rock barricade at the end of the steep and narrow part of Iron Creek Canyon.

To reach the Big Hill trails from the second barricade, continue alongside Iron Creek where the trail becomes a road. After 0.2 mile turn right (north) onto BHNF Road 222-2F which is blocked by a locked gate to prevent motor vehicle access to Big Hill. Climb another 0.4 mile to a small divide and the southern limit of loop D at Big Hill.

To reach the unmarked Red Lake trails from the second barricade, turn left off the main road at the barricade. After 0.1 mile turn left at a wood and gravel barricade across an old road. Follow a faint trail 0.1 mile into a meadow where the trail forks just before reaching a fence. Take the right fork into the trees and begin a steady climb up the nose of a ridge. After crossing a powerline, drop off the southeast side of the ridge. Turn right at a junction 0.9 mile from the barricade and continue for another 0.5 mile to a junction beside an abandoned stock pond. From the stock pond junction the left fork leads another 0.5 mile to a junction which marks the northeast corner of the Red Lake trails.

Fall is the best time of year for this trip. Much of the area is covered by mixed aspen and ponderosa pine. Most overlooks feature patches of golden aspen framed in the dark green of ponderosa pine.

Spearfish Canyon is a botanical crossroads containing species from a wide variety of ecosystems. Low elevation and abundant water combine to produce some of the best conditions in the Black Hills for the development of trees typical of eastern hardwood forests such as birch, aspen, elm, willow, and oak. On cool, shaded north-facing slopes grow white spruce which is a relict of ice age boreal forests. Biologists also recognize more common plants from the Rocky Mountain and Great Plains vegetative regions.

A hike along Iron Creek gives one the sense of what a roadless Spearfish Canyon must have been like. The canyon repelled road builders until the Black Hills gold rush was well under way. It wasn't until 1893 that a railroad from Deadwood to Spearfish penetrated the entire length of the canyon. The railroad provided most of the transportation in the canyon until 1933 when the line, and most of the thirteen bridges along it, were destroyed by flood. The line was replaced by a highway (now U.S. 14A) that uses much of the old railroad bed.

For More Information: Contact Spearfish Ranger District, 2014 N. Main St., Spearfish, SD 57783, (605) 642-4622.

Big Hill Trails

BLACK HILLS NATIONAL FOREST

▲ **Description:** Many loop trips are possible ranging from short, easy family trips to long, difficult tours. The area is best for cross-country skiing and mountain biking.

▲ **General Location:** Eight miles south of Spearfish, South Dakota.

▲ **Access:** From Black Hills State University in Spearfish, drive 0.8 mile west on West Oliver Street, past the Pope and Talbot Sawmill, to the Iron Creek Road (BHNF Road 134). An alternate route to the start of BHNF Road 134 leaves from the junction of North Avenue and Utah in Spearfish. Drive 1.6 miles west on Utah to a four-way stop. From the stop sign drive 0.5 mile south on a gravel road to the start of BHNF Road 134. Drive south on Road 134 for 7.8 miles to the Big Hill Trailhead.

▲ **Distance:** A Loop is the shortest at 2.7 miles and a 10.9-mile loop combines the outer parts of A, C, and D loops.

▲ **Maps:** Black Hills National Forest Big Hill Trails; USGS Maurice, South Dakota, 7.5-minute quadrangle.

Five interconnected loops comprise the Big Hill trails. The trails traverse rolling terrain on the Limestone Plateau west of Spearfish Canyon, through stands of aspen, birch, and ponderosa pine. Big Hill is the most popular area with groomed trails in the Black Hills region. During the winter, Loops A, A1, C, and D are groomed with a track setter by the

Northern Hills Cross-country Ski Club in cooperation with the South Dakota Department of Game, Fish, and Parks and the Black Hills National Forest. Funds for trail maintenance are raised by the club and the Black Hills National Forest, partially through a donation box which is located at the trailhead.

Loop A.1 is 0.6 mile around and is designed primarily as a warm-up trail for skiers. Loop A is the main feeder trail, and is 2 miles around. Loops A and A1 can be combined for an ideal family ski trip. If you are a novice skier, plan on sticking to Loop A on your first trip out. More experienced skiers will use Loop A to access the other trails.

Loop B is 2.2 miles around and a total of 3.6 miles from the trailhead. An overlook offers the best views of Terry Peak and Wharf's Annie Creek Gold Mine possible from Big Hill. This trail is not groomed in the winter for skiing, and therefore less used than the other trails. For mountain bikers, Loop B is also much more challenging. There is more up and down on the loop, and much of it is single track.

At 5.7 miles around and a total of 6.9 miles from the trailhead, Loop C is the longest loop. A short relocation on C, near the junction with C1, was made to bypass a steep hill which was followed by a sharp turn. This relocation may make the start of C1 difficult to find in winter. Trail C1 is a 3-mile round trip to an overlook at the rim of Spearfish Canyon. You can't see very far down into the canyon, but the view extends north to the prairie, and east to Spearfish Peak and Ragged Top. When snow conditions are poor, an exposed ridge on the northern part of C may be bare of snow.

Loop D is 4.5 miles around and a total trip of 7.1 miles from the trailhead. Despite some grueling experiences while cross-country ski racing, it remains one of my favorite ski trails. The snow is usually good and there is a good balance in the length and difficulty of the hills. The meadow around Cabin Springs is a welcome break from the forest on the rest of the trails.

Big Hill is a popular site for cross-country ski racing. Throughout the winter the Northern Hills Cross-country Ski Club sponsors citizens races about every other weekend. Both classic and open technique races are offered. Big Hill is also the site of the Spearfish Challenge, the highlight of the Black Hills racing calendar.

Depending on the route chosen, trips at Big Hill can last from one hour to all day. Skiers should note that all the trails start downhill and the climb out of Eleventh Hour Gulch back to the trailhead is a deceptively long grind. Fit skiers and bikers can combine the outer parts of Loops A, C, and D for a long, but rewarding tour. No water is available along the trail or at the trailhead. There is a latrine in the parking area.

Big Hill is rapidly becoming popular among mountain bikers. With the exception of Loop B, all the trails are relatively smooth two-track dirt roads. The roads are little travelled and closed to motor vehicles year round. On the down side, cattle graze at Big Hill in the summer.

Big Hill trails are well marked, maintained, and easy to follow. All trail junctions are well marked with carsonite posts.

For More Information: Contact Spearfish Ranger District, 2014 N. Main St., Spearfish, SD 57783, (605) 642-4622; or Ski Cross Country, 701 3rd St., Spearfish, SD 57783, (605) 642-3851.

Crow Peak Trail
BLACK HILLS NATIONAL FOREST

- ▲ **Description:** A day hike to the top of Crow Peak along a well-maintained trail.
- ▲ **General Location:** Four miles southwest of Spearfish, South Dakota.
- ▲ **Access:** The Crow Peak Trailhead is located 4 miles south of Spearfish on the Higgins Gulch Road (BHNF Road 214). There is a large parking area with a trail sign and register box on the west side of the road.
- ▲ **Distance:** 7 miles round trip.
- ▲ **Maps:** Black Hills National Forest Map; Crow Peak Trail Map; USGS Maurice, South Dakota, 7.5-minute quadrangle.

Dominating the skyline west of Spearfish is the distinctive double-humped profile of Crow Peak. The Black Hills National Forest has recently constructed a trail for hikers and horseback riders to the top of the peak that captures your eye from Interstate 90.

From Higgins Gulch, the Crow Peak Trail winds west across the lower slopes of the mountain through mixed stands of ponderosa pine, aspen, and birch. A side trail to Beaver Ridge leaves the Crow Peak Trail about half-way up Crow Peak. Reaching the west side of the mountain, the trail climbs up a series of switchbacks and across loose talus slopes to reach the north ridge. The last section of trail stays on the ridge and follows gentler grades south to the summit.

Crow Peak is a popular hike, and justifiably so. The views from the top of the peak are fantastic. Terry Peak, Spearfish Peak, Bear Butte, and Cement Ridge are the most prominent summits. More intriguing perhaps are the Bearlodge Mountains and the Wyoming portion of the Black Hills to the west. Crow Peak may be the best vantage point for scouting Inyan Kara Mountain and other outlying peaks, and is certainly a great spot for photographing them. On clear days, 75 miles to the north, the Slim Buttes and Short Pine Hills are visible.

An ascent of Crow Peak offers an illustration of the effects of different rock types on soils and topography. The lower part of the mountain is

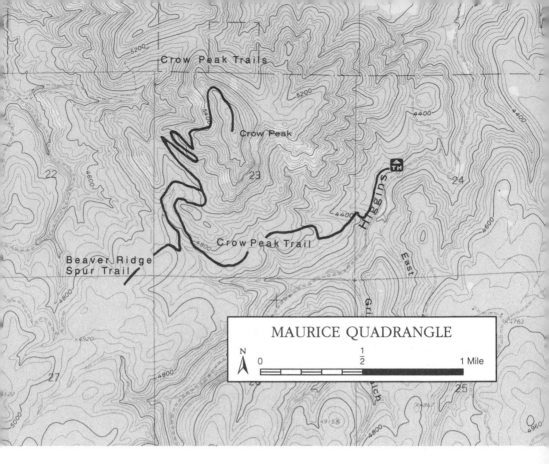

composed of Minnelusa shales and sandstones which are easily eroded to form distinctive red soils and relatively gentle slopes. Farther up the mountain are the lighter colored and more resistant rocks of the Paha Sapa limestone and the Deadwood sandstone which weather to form lighter soils and steeper slopes. The upper core of Crow Peak is quartz latite porphyry, a type of intrusive igneous rock. The porphyry weathers into the coarse plates which compose talus slopes below the summit. The quartz latite is very hard and resistant to erosion, consequently the steepest hiking on Crow Peak is at the end of the climb.

Sixteen hundred feet of elevation gain and numerous switchbacks across talus slopes combine to make this hike moderately strenuous. The hike should take about 4 to 4½ hours round trip. No water or other facilities are available along the trail or at the trailhead.

Hikers should be particularly careful to avoid afternoon thunderstorms on high exposed summits such as Crow Peak. Many hikers have had the dubious pleasure of being pelted with hail and gusts of wind during lightening storms on their retreat from the summit. The best strategy to avoid storms is to start your hike early in the day and take cover or retreat if a storm does arise.

For More Information: Contact Spearfish Ranger District, 2014 N. Main St., Spearfish, SD 57783, (605) 642-4622.

Spearfish Peak

BLACK HILLS NATIONAL FOREST

▲ **Description:** A rugged off-trail hike from the bottom of Spearfish Canyon to the top of Spearfish Peak.
▲ **General Location:** Three miles south of Spearfish, South Dakota.
▲ **Access:** The route starts on U.S. 14A in Spearfish Canyon about one-half mile north of Rimrock Lodge, just past the driveway for a summer cabin. Park on the shoulder of the highway.
▲ **Distance:** About 4 miles round trip with 1,800 feet of elevation gain.
▲ **Maps:** Black Hills National Forest; USGS Spearfish, South Dakota, 7.5-minute quadrangle.

Spearfish Peak is the prominent forested summit on the east rim of Spearfish Canyon. If you think all summits in the Black Hills are easy to reach from any direction, this is one climb that may change your mind.

The ascent requires a topographic map and a willingness to do some scrambling on the way up. The major difficulties are at the start of the trip. Almost all the land in the bottom of the canyon is privately owned and this route starts just north of a cabin, so you should stop and ask permission before beginning your climb.

Cross Spearfish Creek and scramble up a steep, slick slope covered with loose rocks and branches. The first band of limestone cliffs along the route requires a little scrambling, but can be bypassed near the head of a small, southeast trending draw. Beyond this band of cliffs work your way mostly south to reach the crest of the northwest ridge of Spearfish Peak.

Once on the ridge simply follow it to the broad summit. A false peak on the Section 33/34 boundary is just a little beyond the halfway point. If you stay exactly on the ridge crest you will need to climb a few crumbling limestone cliffs, but generally you can get around the cliffs on the north side. To really enjoy the scrambling, and as a safety precaution, it is best to have a partner along on this ascent. The cliffs offer the best views down into the canyon, as the top is relatively flat and wooded. Look for a BHNF survey marker on the summit.

An alternate route for the descent leads southeast off the summit to join a powerline road and then BHNF Road 220. Follow the road south just beyond a shallow saddle at point 5,458. Once beyond the saddle turn into a draw which leads north into the drainage directly south of the peak. A premature exit from the road leads into a draw which heads west and ends at the top of a crumbling, thirty-foot tall cliff. Follow the north draw downhill for about a mile to Rimrock Lodge. From Rimrock Lodge hike north on U.S. 14A back to your starting point.

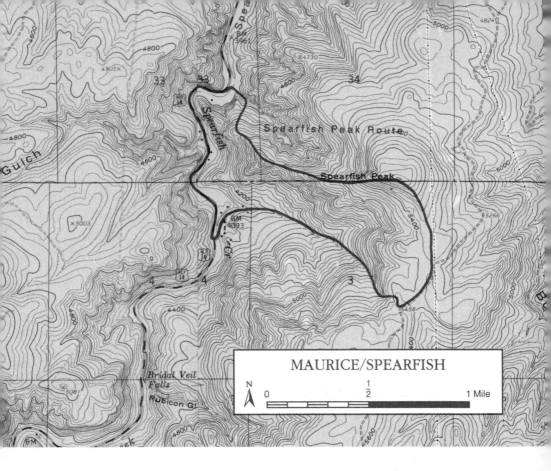

Private land in the bottom of Spearfish Canyon is the major obstacle of this trip. Be sure to respect all rights of property owners to ensure that this challenging route remains open. As with any off-trail hike, carry a topographic map and compass and know how to use them. Scrambling anywhere on the walls of Spearfish Canyon requires experience, common sense, and a healthy respect for the fractured nature of outcrops of Paha Sapa Limestone.

Of course, Spearfish Peak can also be approached from the east side via BHNF Road 220 or by Burno Gulch, which lies only one mile west of the peak.

For More Information: Contact Spearfish Ranger District, 2014 N. Main St., Spearfish, SD 57783, (605) 642-4622.

Burno Gulch

BLACK HILLS NATIONAL FOREST

▲ **Description:** A moderate mountain bike loop trip over jeep trails and gravel roads.
▲ **General Location:** Four miles northwest of Lead, South Dakota.

▲ **Access:** From Lead drive 2.1 miles north on U.S. 14A to the Maitland Road, which is BHNF Road 195. Drive 8.1 miles north on the Maitland Road to the junction of Burno Gulch and False Bottom Creek. Three roads intersect here, the route starts on the middle fork.

▲ **Distance:** A 12.2-mile loop with a 1,400-foot climb.

▲ **Maps:** Black Hills National Forest; USGS Spearfish, South Dakota, 7.5-minute quadrangle.

The small town of Maitland is the starting point for some of the best mountain bike rides in the Black Hills. One favorite loop connects Burno Gulch with False Bottom Creek. To get all your climbing done at the beginning of the loop, and save the downhill ride for the end, start this trip where Burno Gulch joins False Bottom Creek.

From the confluence of Burno Gulch and False Bottom Creek take the middle of the three roads which intersect the Maitland Road. The road passes north of the gulch and south of some houses, but does not cross any locked gates or roads posted "No Trespassing." Follow the dirt road for 0.6 mile on the northwest side of Burno Gulch to a powerline. There is currently logging on this section which extends for another one-quarter of a mile past the powerline.

Beyond the logging area enjoy a steady climb along a two-track dirt road which keeps to the northwest side of Burno Gulch. An unnamed tributary joins Burno Gulch beside a cabin 1.8 miles north of the powerline. A red dirt road follows the tributary, but our route stays left on a jeep trail along the main stem on what a sign soon declares to be "Miller Drive."

The jeep trail follows the powerline for 1.4 miles to a road junction at the confluence with Chism Gulch. Continue to ascend the main fork of Burno Gulch, passing a road on the left after 0.6 mile and a road on the right in another 0.4 mile.

The route turns southeast to leave Burno Gulch 1.2 miles beyond Chism Gulch then climbs for 0.2 mile to a well-maintained dirt road on the Burno–False Bottom divide at 5,679 feet. Take a well-deserved break at the end of this relentless climb, for the rest of the ride will be downhill.

Turn east and follow the divide a short distance, passing a road on the left leading north. Drop into the headwaters of False Bottom Creek passing a small pond and dam after 0.5 mile. After crossing the familiar powerline, turn left onto BHNF Road 186, 1 mile from the divide. Follow Road 186 for 1.4 miles to the junction with gravel BHNF Road 195 in the town of Maitland. Once in Maitland, turn left onto Road 195 and ride north for 4.8 miles back to the mouth of Burno Gulch.

The now quiet town of Maitland was once the site of a roaring gold mining camp. Gold was mined sporadically from 1876 until the mines

were shut down by the U.S. government during World War II. The mines produced 100,000 ounces of gold primarily during the boom times from 1902 to 1915 and during the 1930s. Production came from several thousand feet of drifts linked by shafts which reached to 620 feet deep.

For More Information: Contact Nemo Ranger District, P.O. Box 407, Deadwood, SD 57732, (605) 578-2744.

North Hanna

BLACK HILLS NATIONAL FOREST

▲ **Description:** An easy cross-country ski or mountain bike trip mostly on abandoned forest roads.

▲ **General Location:** Six miles southwest of Lead, South Dakota.

▲ **Access:** From the junction of U.S. 14A and 85 in Lead, drive 5.3 miles southwest on U.S. 85. Park where the Terry Peak Summit Road intersects U.S. 85 and 14A. The route starts a few hundred yards downhill and across the road where Snowmobile Trail 5 enters BHNF Road 549.

▲ **Distance:** The long loop is 5.6 miles around.

▲ **Maps:** Black Hills National Forest; USGS Lead, South Dakota, 7.5-minute quadrangle.

North Hanna is an area of deep snow, gentle terrain, and spectacular vistas that is perfect for cross-country skiing. The proximity to Lead, and the relatively small size of the area, make it ideal for evening or short weekend trips. The numerous open, west-facing ridges are ideal for watching the sun set before returning back home, guided by the lights on top of Terry Peak.

From the start of BHNF Road 549, ski for 0.4 mile on Snowmobile Trail 5 to a road intersection on a ridge. From the ridge, Snowmobile Trail 5 follows BHNF Road 549-1C to Road 627-1A. Our route descends southwest through open timber on Road 549 which is unmarked at this intersection. Follow Road 549 for 0.8 mile, along this north-facing slope with deep snow, to the west end of a small saddle and the junction of BHNF Roads 549.1 and 549.1A. This saddle is marked by a sign for 549.1A.

From the saddle, stay right in an open area and follow BHNF Road 549.1A northwest. Road 549.1A ends after 0.8 mile at a turnaround on a ridge. Skiers can follow this ridge due north to its end on a heavily wooded rim just above Cheyenne Crossing. To continue on the loop, ski south from the turnaround along the ridge crest for 0.7 mile to reach another turnaround which marks the end of BHNF Road 549.1. Mountain bike riders will probably have to push along this ridge crest. Ski

Road 549.1 in a gentle "U" to return to the sign at the 549.1/549.1A junction after 1.5 miles.

To return to the start, skiers can either retrace their route from this point, or ski due east to climb the next ridge. This climb is a steep cross-country route that should only be attempted by experienced skiers. BHNF Road 549.1D follows this ridge north, back to an intersection with Snowmobile Trail 5. The ridge route is more difficult, but offers superior views of Terry Peak and Icebox Gulch to the north. Along with the views, skiers will note the plentiful deer tracks along the ridge.

The North Hanna area is bounded by Icebox Gulch to the north, the Hanna Road to the south and west, and Snowmobile Trail 5 to the east. Snowmobile Trail 5 and BHNF Road 549 provide access into the area. In the summer, the gate across Road 549 at U.S. 85 is closed and motorized vehicles are prohibited in the area. During the snowmobile season, Trail 5 provides motorized access to the area. In any season the area is lightly used and there does not appear to be any skier/snowmobile conflicts.

The route passes through a forest dominated by ponderosa pine. The area was once heavily logged, but is now recovering. Deer and coyotes are common, and numerous standing dead trees provide homes for cavity-nesting birds and small animals.

Due to summer road closures, this is an excellent area to explore on a mountain bike. Bikers should not attempt to ride the ridge south of Road 549.1 which is recommended as a return route for skiers. In addition to the route described here, there a number of other abandoned roads in the area worthy of exploration.

Like many of the other areas in the Black Hills which are good for skiing, North Hanna is part of the Limestone Plateau. Soils developed on the bedrock of Paha Sapa Limestone are rich in clay and break down into thick, sticky gumbo when wet. To avoid the gumbo, try another ride closer to Lead–Deadwood in wet weather.

For More Information: Contact Spearfish Ranger District, 2014 N. Main St., Spearfish, SD 57783, (605) 642-4622.

Black Hills Burlington Northern Heritage Trail
LEAD PROJECT

▲ **Description:** An easy trip along a converted railroad grade.
▲ **General Location:** One mile south of Lead, South Dakota.
▲ **Access:** To reach the Kirk Trailhead, drive 1½ miles east of Lead on the

unpaved Kirk road. Turn south on the unpaved Yellow Creek Road and turn immediately right. Follow a gravel road to the trailhead located on the east bank of Whitewood Creek. The Sugarloaf Trailhead is located about a mile and half south of Lead on U.S. 85.

▲ **Distance:** A 5.5-mile demonstration section is complete.

▲ **Maps:** South Dakota Department of Game, Fish, and Parks Black Hills Burlington Northern Heritage Trail Map; USGS Lead, South Dakota, 7.5-minute quadrangle.

After years of planning and litigation, the Black Hills Burlington Northern Heritage Trail rails to trails conversion is finally beginning. The South Dakota Supreme Court declared the old railway abandoned and upheld the right of the State of South Dakota to use the railbed for public transport. Despite the threat of future appeals, two demonstration projects near Lead and Custer have been completed.

The northern demonstration project was built in 1991 and consists of 5.5 miles of trail south of Lead. This section was dedicated by former South Dakota Governor George Mickelson, who was a strong supporter of the rails to trails project. The route uses two different railroad grades, one along Whitewood Creek and one on Whitetail Summit.

Most people prefer to start their trip at the Kirk Trailhead. From Kirk, head south crossing Whitewood Creek four times across bridges. After 1.9 miles, reach the old Wasp Mine, sand tailings dam, and a dirt road leading south to Englewood. Follow the grade south for 0.4 mile and reach a junction with Snowmobile Trail 7 at the Whitewood Creek Trailhead.

Follow Trail 7 uphill and west for 0.5 mile to the junction of Snowmobile Trails 7 and 5 along another railroad grade. Turn north, and follow this grade for 1.8 miles north to Whitetail Summit. From here, continue downhill 0.9 mile to U.S. 85 and the Sugarloaf Trailhead.

Although this is a new trail, it is already one of the most popular in the Black Hills. The trail is used in midweek by local residents and is starting to attract mountain bikers from farther away on the weekends. Despite this use, expect to see deer along the trail and wild turkeys along Whitetail Summit in the spring and fall.

The Black Hills Burlington Northern Heritage Trail has already proven to be one of the best cross-country ski trails in the Black Hills for beginning skiers. The trail is excellent for skiing; the flat railroad bed is broken only by three crossings of Whitewood Creek. From Kirk to Englewood, the trail is in a deep valley which collects snow and is protected from afternoon snowmelt. Reconstruction of the trail resulted in a very smooth surface, so the trail can be skied even with minimal snow cover.

From Englewood to U.S. 85, the ski trail is part of the Black Hills snowmobile trail system. Snowmobiles are allowed on this part of the

LEAD QUADRANGLE

trail from December 1 to March 31. Competition from snowmobiles, and the steady climb to Whitetail Summit from either Whitetail Creek or U.S. 85, make this segment less attractive for beginning skiers. However, more experienced skiers may find this section ideal for practicing their skating technique on the groomed trail. Skiing is permitted elsewhere on the Black Hills snowmobile trail system, but is not recommended due to heavy snow machine traffic.

The trail will eventually extend 104 miles from Deadwood to Edgemont. In the meantime, the South Dakota Department of Game, Fish, and Parks has a lot of work ahead. Paramount is the requirement that the right-of-way adjacent to private property be fenced before the railway is used as a public trail. Missing trestles and bridges along the route present significant safety hazards. Although much of the railway is currently accessible to hikers and bikers, Game, Fish, and Parks discourages use of unopened parts of the trail because of safety concerns, and the fear of damaging already strained relationships with private landowners along the route. Maps of the trail are displayed on signboards at the trailheads. Picnic tables have been placed at all trailheads, at the Homestake Overlook, and at Creekside Rest. The project is designed for non-motorized recreation and will be wheelchair accessible.

For More Information: Contact South Dakota Department of Game, Fish, and Parks, 523 E. Capitol, Pierre, SD 57501, (605) 773-3391; or Black Hills Rails to Trails Association, Box 777 South Junction Ave., Sturgis, SD 57785, (605) 347-3604.

Deer Mountain Cross-country Ski Trails

▲ **Description:** An easy cross-country ski tour on groomed trails. Deer Mountain is a private ski area and charges a fee for trail users.
▲ **General Location:** Three miles south of Lead, South Dakota.
▲ **Access:** Drive 3 miles southwest of Lead on U.S. 85 and 14A to the sign for the Deer Mountain Ski Area. Follow the gravel entrance road west to the upper parking area at the base of the ski area.
▲ **Distance:** A 3-mile loop.
▲ **Maps:** Deer Mountain Cross-country and Touring Trail Map; USGS Lead, South Dakota, 7.5-minute quadrangle.

Many Black Hills skiers get their introduction to cross country on the trail system at Deer Mountain. Groomed trails, deep-set tracks, and the gentle terrain along the railroad grade are ideal for novices and for those looking to polish their diagonal stride.

To make your trip easier, pick up a trail map at the lodge building before heading out on the five-kilometer loop. The cross-country trails start to the right of the ski lodge at the upper parking lot. The loop is best skied counterclockwise to break up the long climb back to the trailhead.

The Deer Mountain Trail starts with two sharp drops before making a fast run down into Campground Meadow. After 0.9 mile at the bottom of the meadow, turn left back up the meadow staying on the Deer Mountain Trail. After 1.5 miles reach the Railroad Grade Trail and turn left onto the grade. At 1.7 miles turn left off the grade onto the Golden Reward Trail. From this intersection ambitious skiers can add an additional 1.6 miles to the loop by continuing on the Railroad Grade Trail and then returning via the ungroomed Buck Ridge Trail.

To return to the parking area from the beginning of the Golden Reward Trail, turn left at the junction of the Golden Reward and Buck Ridge trails. At 2.1 miles, turn right onto the Deer Mountain Trail and climb steadily back to the start.

Deer Mountain charges $4 for a day pass to cover grooming costs. A season pass for cross-country skiing costs $50. Trails are groomed depending on snow conditions. A cross-country ski package can be rented for the day for $6.50 and a two-hour lesson at the area costs $8.50.

For More Information: Contact Deer Mountain Ski Area, P.O. Box 662, Deadwood, SD 57732, (605) 584-3230.

Dutch Flats
BLACK HILLS NATIONAL FOREST

▲ **Description:** An easy mountain bike ride or cross-country ski trip with many side trips to overlooks above Spearfish Canyon.
▲ **General Location:** Six miles west of Lead, South Dakota.
▲ **Access:** From Lead, drive one mile west on U.S. 85 to the Terry Peak Road. Drive west on the Terry Peak Road to the end of pavement, then turn left onto a gravel road. Drive 0.6 mile on the gravel road past the Terry Peak Ski Area to Deep Snow Trail. Park at a locked gate across BHNF Road 629.
▲ **Distance:** 6.8 miles round trip to the overlook above Elmore or 4.7 miles for Leroy's Loop.
▲ **Maps:** Black Hills National Forest; USGS Lead and Savoy, South Dakota, 7.5-minute quadrangles.

Dutch Flats is a high, isolated plateau located between Spearfish Canyon, Icebox Gulch, Terry Peak, and Wharf's Annie Creek Mine. BHNF Road 629 and its subsidiary roads are closed to motor vehicles,

SAVOY/LEAD QUADRANGLES

N

0      $\frac{1}{2}$ 1 Mile

Terry Peak

Lookout Tower

Radio Tower

Overlook Route

BLACK

Gulch

Sweet Betsey Gulch

10

Dutch Flats

Dutch Flats Routes

629.1A

Leroy's Loop

Overlook

Spearfish Creek

HILL

Raspberry Gulch

15

14

Icebox

Cheyenne Crossing

North Hanna Routes

AQUEDUCT

22

23

BM 5622

Gulch

USFS 549.1A

USFS 549.1

USFS 549.1D

USFS 549.1C

N

A

T

I

O

N

A

L

27

26

Hanna Road

Wildcat Gulch

Hanna Campground

but offer access to superb overlooks for hikers, mountain bikers, and cross-country skiers.

A locked gate across BHNF Road 629 marks the start of the trip. Begin with a 1.3-mile descent to Dutch Flats and a major T-junction located just past Dutch Flats Spring. From the T-junction two different trips are possible.

The right fork follows a ridge to an overlook above Elmore. One-tenth of a mile beyond the T-junction, a grassy road leads north into Lost Camp Gulch. After another 0.5 mile, BHNF Road 629.1E leads south from the head of Sweet Betsy Gulch. Continue west along the ridge for another 1.4 miles to the end of the road. For a great view down into Spearfish Canyon and the old town of Elmore, climb the ridge to the west.

From the T-junction the left fork leads 0.3 mile on BHNF Road 629.1A to Leroy's Loop, which begins at the 1A/1B intersection. To complete the loop, head south 0.4 mile on rapidly deteriorating Road 629.1A to the west end of ridge 6,196. From the crest of the ridge a side trail leads 0.3 mile to an overlook above heavily forested Raspberry Gulch. Continue north on the ridge 0.3 mile, passing a turkey guzzler, to a four-way junction.

From the four-way junction BHNF Road 629.1D leads west 0.5 mile to an overlook above Spearfish Canyon. Road 629.1C leads left 0.5 mile southeast to a dead end. To continue on Leroy's Loop, turn right (east) at the four-way junction and follow 629.1C for 0.6 mile to a junction with Road 629.1B. Continue straight at the 1B/1C junction and turn left at the end of the loop to return to the T-junction.

Dutch Flats is equally interesting on a mountain bike or cross-country skis. The main road to Dutch Flats Spring is intermittently gravelled, but otherwise the roads are relatively smooth, overgrown two-track dirt roads ideal for bikes. Not all the roads have signs, so carry a map for navigation. There has been no grazing at Dutch Flats since 1990 so the meadow around Dutch Flats Spring is surprisingly lush. Expect to see plenty of deer here in the summer.

The elevation at Dutch Flats ranges from 5,900 to 6,400 feet so the area receives deep snow. The tree cover is dense enough to shade the trails, but open enough so that the tree canopy doesn't intercept all the snow. Skiers should note that snowmobiles also use Dutch Flats.

There is only one drawback to a trip to Dutch Flats. The climb from Dutch Flats Spring to the gate at the start is long and unrelenting. Don't expend too much energy exploring all the side trail and overlooks and save a little for the trip out.

For More Information: Contact Spearfish Ranger District, 2014 N. Main St., Spearfish, SD 57783, (605) 642-4622.

Pillar Peak

BLACK HILLS NATIONAL FOREST

▲ **Description:** A moderate cross-country ski or mountain bike trip from Galena which finishes with a short hike to the top of Pillar Peak.

▲ **General Location:** Five miles east of Deadwood, South Dakota.

▲ **Access:** To reach Galena, drive south from Pluma 5.2 miles and turn off U.S. 385 onto BHNF Road 534. Drive 4 miles to a bridge across Bear Butte Creek. Park on the roadside by the bridge.

▲ **Distance:** 3.3 miles one way by bike or ski, and one-half mile of hiking to Pillar Peak.

▲ **Maps:** Black Hills National Forest; USGS Deadwood South, South Dakota, 7.5-minute quadrangle.

The town of Galena is a convenient starting point for exploring the northeast corner of the Black Hills, an area of rugged canyons and relatively low summits. Pillar Peak, one of the most interesting of these summits, can be reached via a four-mile long trip through an area seldom travelled.

From the bridge over Bear Butte Creek, head up Butcher Gulch for a quarter of a mile. Leave Butcher Gulch at a sharp switchback to the right, and climb steadily to the nose of a prominent ridge overlooking Galena from the north. Beyond Butcher Gulch, the route is entirely on Black Hills National Forest land. Follow the ridge northwest to a saddle on the southwest shoulder of Bear Den Mountain which is one mile from Galena.

Descend from the saddle to reach BHNF Road 172 in the valley of Lost Gulch. Pass the remains of an old cabin after 1.8 miles, then turn northwest onto BHNF Road 172-1C at a point 2.3 miles from Galena. Climb steadily along brush-covered Road 172-1C to reach another saddle after 2.7 miles. Then follow the road along contour to a third saddle located on the southeast shoulder of Pillar Peak. This saddle is 3.3 miles from Galena.

The last half-mile to the top of Pillar Peak is steep, rocky, and without a trail. Skiers with new skis, or those lacking confidence in their ability to turn among the trees and rocks, may elect to walk the upper slope to the summit.

Pillar Peak may have the best views in the northeast corner of the Black Hills; if not, at least you can see all the likely contenders from there. To the northeast is Bear Butte and to the north Whitewood Peak and Crook Mountain are particularly prominent. Mount Theodore Roosevelt, Terry Peak, Deer Mountain, and Custer Peak surround the Lead-Deadwood area. Those unfamiliar with this part of the hills are struck

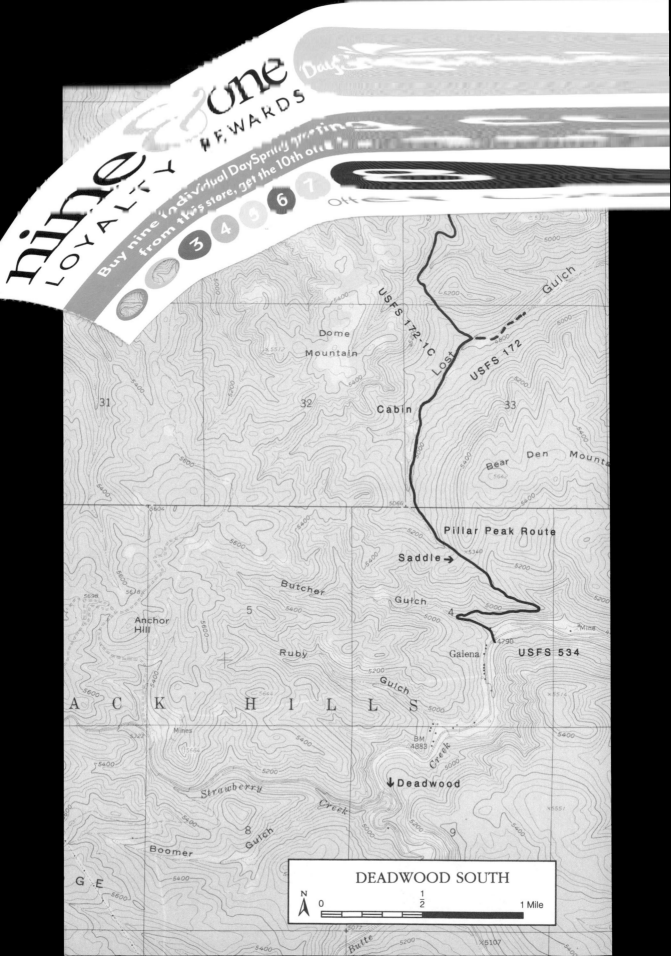

by the deep, rugged canyons draining the northern flank. Once you've planned a few more trips from this scenic spot, it is time to return to Galena by retracing your route.

The first discovery of silver in the northeast Black Hills occurred in March, 1876. By January 1877, a town of seventy-five buildings housed four hundred miners. The town was named Galena for the silver-bearing lead sulfide mineral which contained most of the ore in the district. Large-scale mining began in the area in 1878 with the opening of the Florence Mine by J. H. Davy, and the town has since endured numerous boom and bust cycles typical of mining camps.

The reopening of the Branch Mint Mine by J. D. Hardin signalled a second burst of mining which lasted from 1904 to 1912. The most recent attempt at profitable silver mining at Galena was at the Double Rainbow Mine operated by Homestake Mining Company. The Double Rainbow headframe is just downstream from the bridge over Bear Butte Creek on the right side of the road.

The recent gold mining boom in the Black Hills has also touched Galena. Just up Strawberry Creek from Bear Butte Creek is the Gilt Edge Gold Mine. After nearly twenty years of intermittent exploration, the Gilt Edge Mine opened in 1987 as an open pit/heap leach operation.

BHNF Road 172 is open, but not maintained, in the winter. When snow conditions permit, the route is an excellent introduction to the potential for cross-country ski climbs of Black Hills summits. Snowmobiles and some vehicles may travel partway up the road along Lost Gulch. However, the area is lightly travelled except during hunting season, and skiers can expect to be alone and to break trail.

Several other possible routes exist in the Galena area including trips up Bear Den Mountain or Anchor Hill, and a loop which connects Butcher Gulch with the unnamed gulch that starts at the abandoned cabin.

For More Information: Contact Nemo Ranger District, P.O. Box 407, Deadwood, SD 57732, (605) 578-2744.

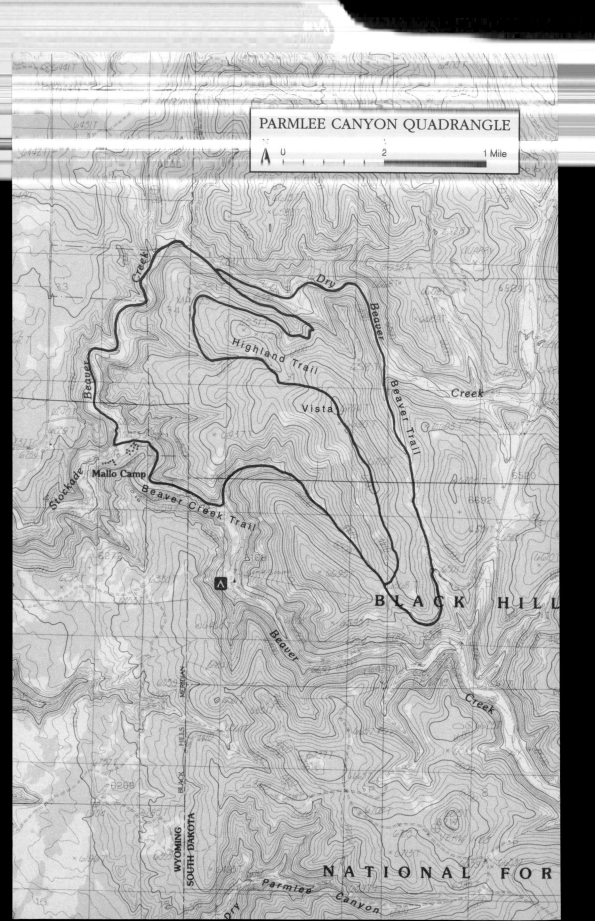

PARMLEE CANYON QUADRANGLE

N

0   2   1 Mile

Dry

Beaver

Creek

Creek

Highland Trail

Beaver Trail

Vista

Stockade

Mallo Camp

Beaver Creek Trail

BLACK HILL

6692

Beaver

Creek

MERIDIAN

BLACK HILLS

WYOMING
SOUTH DAKOTA

Dry

Parmlee   Canyon

NATIONAL   FOR

WYOMING

Beaver Creek Cross-country Ski Trails
BLACK HILLS NATIONAL FOREST

▲ **Description:** A moderate cross-country ski or mountain bike trip.
▲ **General Location:** Four miles east of Four Corners, Wyoming.
▲ **Access:** From Lead, South Dakota, drive 34 miles southwest on U.S. 85 to Four Corners, Wyoming. Drive 4.7 miles east on the Mallo Road (BHNF Road 810) to the junction with BHNF Road 111 at a parking area. There is a trail sign at the top of the hill. If road conditions permit, drive 0.6 mile down a steep hill to Mallo Camp and park in a turnout adjacent to the trail register.
▲ **Distance:** The Highland Trail loop is 7.7 miles around.
▲ **Maps:** Black Hills National Forest Beaver Creek Ski Trails; USGS Parmlee, Wyoming–South Dakota, 7.5-minute quadrangle.

Tucked far off the beaten track of Black Hills skiing is the Beaver Creek Ski Area. If you are tired of seeing the same groups at popular areas such as Eagle Cliff or Big Hill, Beaver Creek offers a chance for solitude without compromising snow conditions or trail quality.

Beaver Creek is located on the western flank of the Black Hills along the South Dakota-Wyoming border. The area is high enough to receive, and hold, deep snowfalls. The topography and elevation make Beaver Creek ski conditions very similar to those at Eagle Cliff.

The trail system is designed so that most skiers travel one of three loops. The trail over Highland Ridge is the most interesting and most used. To ski the Highland Loop, proceed north from Mallo Camp through open meadows along Dry Beaver Creek. The trail crosses private land on the Wyoming side of the border, so be careful not to leave any signs of your passage. At point "G," and the junction with BHNF Road 712, turn southwest up a small side drainage. Look for a switchback where the trail leaves this draw. Then, wrap around the northeast end of Highland Ridge, just skirting the Wyoming line, and then climb east to the open meadow and vista near the top of Highland Ridge.

At Highland Ridge, stop for lunch and enjoy the views of the little-travelled western flank of the Black Hills. When you become more cold than hungry, it is time to enjoy the rewards of your morning climb with a gradual ridgeline descent toward Beaver Creek. At point "D" turn northeast to follow a side draw to point "B" and BHNF Road 111. Follow Road 111 back to Mallo Camp.

Beaver Creek trails are easy to follow. The trails are marked by blue plastic diamonds on trees, and trail junctions are lettered and marked with brown carsonite posts. Since the area is little used, you can expect to break trail, so bring some friends along to help share the work and the fun.

From Mallo Camp to the Beaver Creek Campground, skiers share the trail with snowmobiles. If you ski this section, be especially careful and step to the side of the trail to allow snowmobiles to pass. Unfortunately, some of the other ski trails are also used illegally by snowmobiles. Copies of the trail map may be stored in the register box.

For More Information: Contact Elk Mountain Ranger District, 640 South Summit, Newcastle, WY 82701, (307) 746-2783.

Sand Creek

BLACK HILLS NATIONAL FOREST

▲ **Description:** A moderately difficult off-trail hike through steep canyons in the northwestern corner of the Black Hills.
▲ **General Location:** Eight miles south of Beulah, Wyoming.
▲ **Access:** From Interstate 90, take Exit 205 and follow the signs south to the Ranch A Fish Hatchery. Pass Ranch A 7.3 miles beyond I-90, and the Black Hills National Forest boundary after 9 miles. Once in the Black Hills National Forest, the road becomes number 863. At 13.9 miles reach Bridge 302 over Sand Creek and a small turnout on the right side suitable for parking.
▲ **Distance:** The short loop is approximately 4 miles long.
▲ **Maps:** Black Hills National Forest; USGS Tinton and Red Canyon Creek, Wyoming–South Dakota, 7.5-minute quadrangles.

Sand Creek is perhaps the most botanically diverse part of the Black Hills. The area is wild, rugged, and little travelled. No maintained trails exist, and the only roads are abandoned, overgrown relics of small, early mining and logging operations. Creek bottoms and the abandoned roadways are the best means of travel through Sand Creek. The creek bottoms are usually dry and reasonably clear of vegetation.

RED CANYON/TINTON

From the bridge over Sand Creek on BHNF Road 863, hike one mile up the cobble-strewn creek bottom to the confluence with Corral Creek. A now-collapsed cabin once sat here on a small bench above the creeks. Continue to follow Sand Creek upstream to the east for a short distance until a narrow, overgrown tract begins to climb the south wall of the canyon.

About half way up the canyon wall the tract fades away. Bushwack (literally) up the slope to a flat ridge which divides Sand and Corral creeks. At an elevation of about 4,800 feet on this ridge, there is the remains of an old roadway which offers easy walking along contour. Follow the roadway for about three-quarters of a mile along the top of a resistant, cliff-forming bed of limestone. Just before reaching a major west-flowing tributary of Corral Creek, scramble down the cliffs and through the woods to Corral Creek. Once in the bed of Corral Creek continue downstream for about a mile back to the confluence with Sand Creek. From the confluence, retrace your route back along Sand Creek to the bridge and BHNF Road 863.

Sand Creek is one of the largest roadless areas remaining in the Black Hills. Because of its large size, a very long day hike, or overnight back-pack trip is possible. To make the longer loop, continue along Sand Creek four miles beyond the confluence with Corral Creek to Sand Creek Crossing. From the crossing, hike west over a small ridge into the head-waters of Corral Creek. Depending on where you enter Corral Creek, it is about four miles back along the creek bottom to Sand Creek.

Even to the amateur the diversity of the boreal (northern) forest of Sand Creek is a striking contrast to the ponderosa pine-dominated forest typical of the Black Hills. Cool, moist conditions allow this north-ern forest to prosper on the north-facing slopes. Paper birch and hazel-nut are key indicator species, but quaking aspen, spruce, and burr oak are also common.

The boreal forests are a remnant of the northern forests which advanced south during the last ice age. The remaining pockets of this forest, such as Sand Creek, contain a variety of rare plants. Sword fern, club moss, moschatel, and mite wort are a few of the isolated species found along Sand Creek.

Springtime brings an explosion of wildflowers to the creek bottoms and slopes of the canyons. Buttercups, larkspur, blue flax, geraniums, violets, and even the lowly hound's tongue brighten the valleys. The Nature Conservancy, a non-profit organization dedicated to preserving rare and endangered ecosystems, recognized that Sand Creek is the most important area in the Black Hills for rare plants. The Conservancy is pur-suing a special botanical area designation for parts of the drainage.

The Black Hills National Forest is currently rewriting the Forest Plan, its guiding document. As part of the Forest Plan revision process, 7,500 acres around Sand Creek were identified as potential wilderness. A proposal by the Black Hills Group of the Sierra Club, and other conservation groups, recommended that 8,300 acres around Sand Creek be designated wilderness. Much of the area is old growth, but logging is impractical due to numerous limestone cliffs and generally steep slopes. Currently, the Sand Creek area is used primarily for recreation and wildlife habitat.

For More Information: Contact Bearlodge Ranger District, P.O. Box 680, Sundance, WY 82729, (307) 283-1361.

Bearlodge Cross-country Ski Trails
BLACK HILLS NATIONAL FOREST

▲ **Description:** A moderate cross-country ski trip on groomed trails suitable for mountain bikes in summer.
▲ **General Location:** Three miles northwest of Sundance, Wyoming.
▲ **Access:** To reach the trailhead from Interstate 90, take Exit 185 west of Sundance, and drive west on U.S. 14 for one mile. Turn north on BHNF Road 838 (the Warren Peak Road). Drive 2½ miles to the parking area at the end of the plowed road. The trail starts up the paved main road, which is used as a snowmobile trail.
▲ **Distance:** The short loop is 5 miles around.
▲ **Maps:** Black Hills National Forest Bearlodge Cross-country Ski Trails; USGS Sundance NW, Wyoming, 7.5-minute quadrangle.

North of Sundance, near Reuter Campground, lies a network of groomed ski trails centered around Carson Draw. Beautiful trails, a variety of terrain and views stretching across the Bearlodge Mountains to Sundance and Inyan Kara mountains make this trail system one of the undiscovered gems of Black Hills cross-country skiing. The trail system consists of one main loop and a series of spur trails radiating away from the loop. An ungroomed trail in upper Carson Draw allows skiers to make a longer, more difficult loop.

For an introduction to Bearlodge skiing, try a loop around Carson Draw. From the parking area, ski up the Warren Peak Road to post 1, which is located just before the first curve. Beyond this point snowmobiles are not allowed on the ski trails. By veering south off the trail between posts 1 and 2, skiers are treated to impressive views south to Sundance and Inyan Kara mountains. Both peaks are part of a chain of

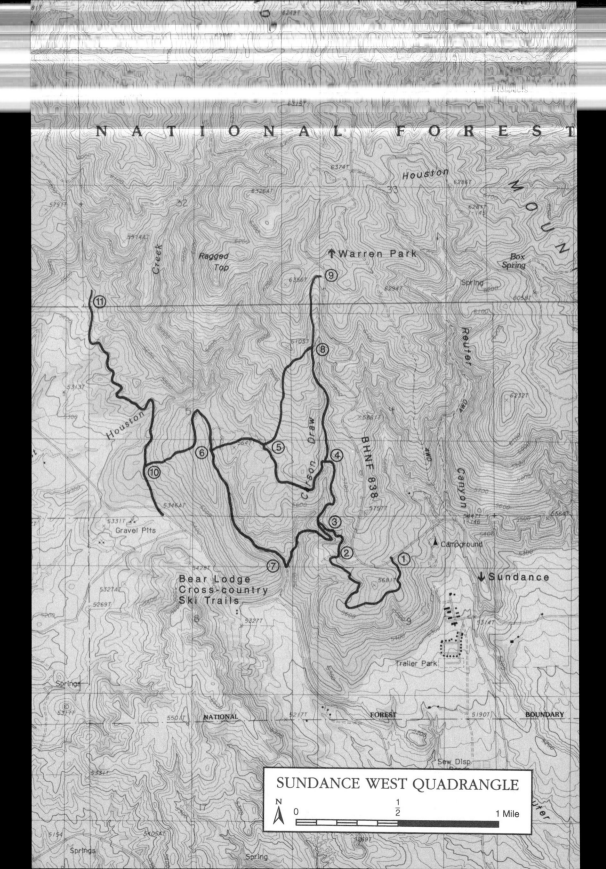

SUNDANCE WEST QUADRANGLE

eroded volcanic centers that cut across the northern Black Hills from Devils Tower to Bear Butte.

Follow a gentle trail north to post 3, where the loop begins. To ascend the steeper hills, and descend the more moderate grades, turn right and follow the loop counterclockwise. A steady ascent soon brings skiers to post 4. From post 4, the ski shelter at post 5 can be reached directly by an easy traverse, or skiers can choose a longer, but more interesting route via post 8. For the longer route, follow the ungroomed trail directly up Carson Draw to post 8. Then turn left for a difficult descent down to the ski shelter.

After enjoying a rest and some lunch at the shelter, ski to the trail junction at post 5. To return to the trailhead, ski downhill to post 7, first through an open meadow, then in a tighter, steeper canyon. Be careful not to build up too much speed. The steep, shaded canyon between posts 6 and 7 is the most exciting skiing within the trail system, as well as one of the most scenic sections. From post 7 climb steeply back to post 3, then return to the trailhead via posts 2 and 1.

Trails are groomed after each snowfall as part of a cooperative agreement between the Black Hills National Forest and the Wyoming Department of Parks and Recreation. Ski tracks are set. Trails are marked by blue diamond-shaped markers and trail intersections are marked by numbered posts.

The terrain within the system offers trails for beginners to advanced skiers. The difficulty ratings on the map issued by the Black Hills National Forest are accurate. Grooming ensures that downhill runs are fast, and some of the most difficult trails can be treacherous if icy. Although the trails are not groomed specifically for skating, the terrain and sugary snow ensure that the trails are perfect for this technique. The trail between posts 4 and 8 is not groomed, and much less used than the other trails.

The BHNF plans to expand the ski trail system by adding ski trails on the east side of the Warren Peak Road. In summer, the ski trail route via points 1, 3, 4, 5, 8, and 9 are used as part of the 22-mile-long Bearlodge Mountain Bike Trails. Part of the mountain bike trails already connects to the Sundance Horse Trails now under construction in the Sundance Burn.

There is no water along the trails, although hikers and mountain bike riders using the trails in the summer can get water at Reuter Campground, located near the trailhead.

For More Information: Contact Bearlodge Ranger District, P.O. Box 680, Sundance, WY 87729, (307) 283-1361.

Cliff Swallow Trail
BLACK HILLS NATIONAL FOREST

▲ **Description:** An easy loop trail through the Bearlodge Mountains.
▲ **General Location:** Twenty miles north of Sundance, Wyoming.
▲ **Access:** From Interstate 90, take Exit 199 and drive north on Wyoming 111 for 4.2 miles. Turn west onto gravel BHNF Road 843 and drive 10.5 miles to gravel BHNF Road 842. Follow Road 842 northwest for 1.2 miles to Cook Lake Recreation Area and continue for 0.5 mile toward campground loop B to a hikers' parking area. The trail starts 100 yards up the road and across from an outhouse.
▲ **Distance:** A 3.5-mile loop.
▲ **Maps:** Black Hills National Forest Cliff Swallow Trail Recreation Opportunity Guide; USGS Black Hills, Wyoming, 7.5-minute quadrangle.

In contrast to the Black Hills, Wyoming's Bearlodge Mountains are little used by hikers. A new trail at the popular recreation area at Cook Lake, in the heart of the Bearlodge, may help hikers to discover this area. The trail was completed in 1991 and offers hikers and mountain bikers an excellent chance to explore the Bearlodge off-road.

From the trailhead, climb on switchbacks to campground loop B. The Cliff Swallow Trail follows the campground road a short distance, then enters the woods near site 28, where there is a large trail sign and map. Cross through a gate in a fence and traverse uphill along the side of a steep ridge. After another set of switchbacks, the trail crosses bluffs of brown sandstone and crests the ridge.

The Cliff Swallow Trail follows the ridge for almost a mile before descending again on switchbacks to a saddle which is crossed by numerous cattle tracks. Be careful to stay on the hiking trail as it turns southeast and crosses a gate in a fence just before reaching the valley of lower Beaver Creek. The trail follows Beaver Creek on a bluff on the northwest side back to the campground road. Near the Cook Lake Dam are several large beaver dams, which seemingly threaten to flood the end of the trail. The trail intersects the campground road about 100 feet from the parking area adjacent to another large trail sign and map.

The Cliff Swallow Trail is an excellent place to study the effects of topography on forest composition. The Bearlodge forests contain a mix of western climax conifers and eastern deciduous trees. The eastern slope of the ridge is covered with a mixture of ponderosa pine and burr oak. Pine dominates the canopy, while oak is most abundant in the understory. On the ridge crest, pine is interspersed with stands of aspen. To the north, the pine-covered ridge has many snags (standing dead trees) and birds are more abundant. The Black Hills National Forest has

BLACK HILLS QUADRANGLE

inventoried twenty-three bird and ten mammal species that depend on snags, and the cavities in them, for shelter. The cliff swallow is not one of these species. These birds nest in the sandstone bluffs just below the top of the ridge.

The Cliff Swallow Trail is marked by carsonite posts and a well-travelled footway. This is one of the few hiking trails in the Black Hills National Forest that was constructed for hiking and mountain biking and is not a converted roadway. Although there is plenty of water in lower Beaver Creek, cattle graze in most of the watershed. During the summer get your drinking water from the campground.

Along with two camping areas and nonmotorized boating at the recreation area, there is also a one-mile loop trail which goes around the lake. Hikers with a little extra time and energy to spend will find this loop relaxing.

For More Information: Contact Bearlodge Ranger District, P.O. Box 680, Sundance, WY 82729, (307) 283-1361.

Joyner Ridge Trail
DEVILS TOWER NATIONAL MONUMENT

▲ **Description:** An easy loop trail suitable for families with small children.
▲ **General Location:** Twenty-two miles northwest of Sundance, Wyoming.
▲ **Access:** From the west side of Sundance, Wyoming, exit Interstate 90 onto U.S. 14. Follow U.S. 14 north for twenty-two miles to Devils Tower Junction. At the junction, turn north on U.S. 24 to reach the Devils Tower National Monument Entrance Station. Follow the park road for 2.3 miles to a paved, unmarked road leading north. The Joyner Ridge Trailhead is 0.3 mile farther north.
▲ **Distance:** The loop is 1.5 miles around.
▲ **Maps:** Devils Tower National Monument Map; USGS Devils Tower, Wyoming, 7.5-minute quadrangle.

Many visitors to Devils Tower are content to view the tower from the park's roads and visitor center. Others will hike around the tower on the paved, one-mile-long Tower Trail. The sheer number of visitors to the Tower ensures that the Tower Trail is one of the most heavily used trails in the Black Hills region. To escape the masses, and enjoy spectacular views of Devils Tower from the north, try a hike along the little-used Joyner Ridge Trail.

To hike the loop clockwise, start from the north side of the parking area. The trail traverses east along a ridge of Sundance formation

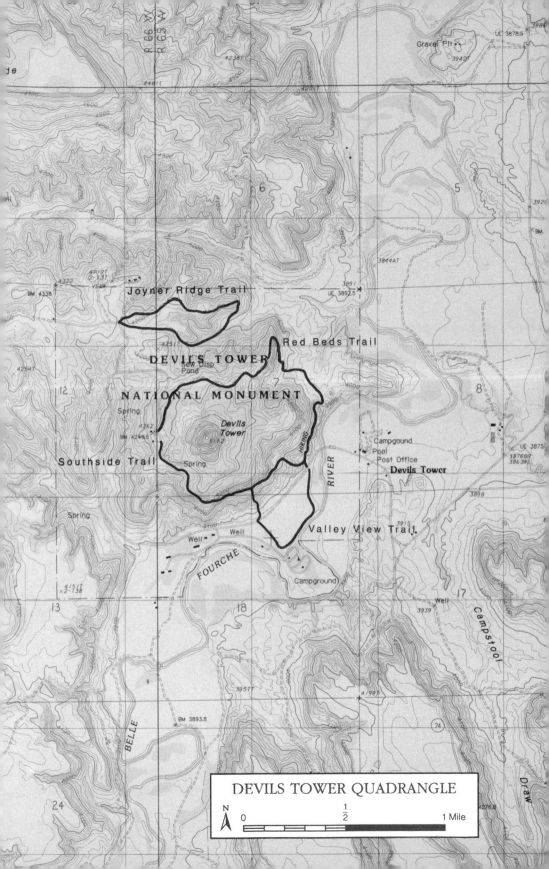

Joyner Ridge Trail

Red Beds Trail

DEVILS TOWER

NATIONAL MONUMENT

Spring

Devils
Tower
5112

Southside Trail

Spring

Campground
Pool
Post Office

Devils Tower

Valley View Trail

Well   Well

FOURCHE

Campground

Well

BELLE

BM 3893.8

DRAW

DEVILS TOWER QUADRANGLE

N   0   ½   1 Mile

sandstone through a forest of ponderosa pine, generally staying within view of Devils Tower. From the east end of the ridge, the trail descends on switchbacks to a juniper-filled ravine. The trail climbs gradually out of the ravine through a forest of burr oak and ash to reach the grasslands near the parking area.

The Joyner Ridge Trail has a well-defined footway, but no blazes. Four interpretive signs along the route highlight aspects of the monument's ecology. Since this trail is much less travelled than the Tower Trail, hikers have a better chance to see white tail deer or one of the 130 bird species which have been sighted within the monument.

No water is found along the trail. Bring a canteen and sun protection, as well as your camera. In summer be prepared for sudden, often violent afternoon thunderstorms. Mountain bikes are not allowed on trails at Devils Tower.

The trail is named for former Monument Superintendent Newell F. Joyner. Joyner's tenure at Devils Tower coincided with the opening of the tower to rock climbing.

For More Information: Contact Devils Tower National Monument, P.O. Box 8, Devils Tower, WY 82714, (307) 467-5501.

Red Beds–Southside Trails Loop
DEVILS TOWER NATIONAL MONUMENT

▲ **Description:** A beautiful loop trail which circles Devils Tower.
▲ **General Location:** Twenty-two miles northwest of Sundance, Wyoming.
▲ **Access:** From the west side of Sundance, exit Interstate 90 onto U.S. 14. Follow U.S. 14 north for twenty-two miles to Devils Tower Junction. At the junction turn north on U.S. 24 to reach the Devils Tower National Monument Entrance Station. From the entrance, drive 2.8 miles to the visitors center.
▲ **Distance:** The loop is 2.8 miles long.
▲ **Maps:** Devils Tower National Monument Map; USGS Devils Tower, Wyoming, 7.5-minute quadrangle.

Devils Tower is one of the most recognizable landmarks in the United States. The tower has been made famous by countless photographs and by the film *Close Encounters of the Third Kind.* Devils Tower and the nearby Missouri Buttes comprise the last gasp of the Black Hills uplift as it fades westward into the prairie of the Thunder Basin.

You don't have to be a rock climber to enjoy a visit to the monument. Three hiking trails circle around the Tower Trail and explore the flanks of the tower along the Belle Fourche River. The Southside Trail starts at the south end of the visitors center parking loop. The trail winds gradually downhill through ponderosa pine, burr oak, and juniper for one-half mile to a junction. From the junction, the Valley View Trail leads south to the campground, and the Red Beds Trail continues the loop around the tower.

The Red Beds Trail skirts a bluff formed from brown sandstone of the Hulett member of the Jurassic Age Sundance formation. Below the rocks of the Sundance formation are the massive white gypsum beds of the Gypsum Springs formation and the bright red sandstone and siltstone of the Triassic Age Spearfish formation. At the bottom of the bluffs, almost at the base of the tower, is another junction with the Valley View Trail. From the intersection, the trail turns north and passes through a sparsely vegetated badlands of easily eroded Spearfish formation.

The Red Beds Trail next reaches grasslands and then traverses a small northeast trending ridge which offers good views of Devils Tower. Rounding the ridge, the trail heads south, then turns west onto an old road bed. The loop ends at the Tower Trail about a hundred feet from the parking area.

Mateo Tepee or "Bear Lodge" is an Indian name for Devils Tower. The scientific party of Colonel Richard Dodge was the first white group to describe Devils Tower and give it the current name. Dodge's party was as awed by the tower as any of the millions of later visitors. They described it as unclimbable.

The label "unclimbable" only serves as a challenge for some. In 1893, local ranchers William Rogers and Willard Ripley made the first ascent of Devils Tower using a ladder they constructed by driving wooden pegs into a vertical crack between two of the columns. The last known climb using the ladder was made by Babe White (known as the "Human Fly"). The park service then removed the lower one hundred feet of the ladder.

Modern rock climbing techniques were first successfully applied to Devils Tower by a three-man team led by the renowned climber Fritz Weissner in 1937. The classic, and easiest, route to the top was pioneered the next year by Jack Durance. The Durance route begins at the "leaning column" and is clearly visible on the cover of *Geology of Devils Tower—The First National Monument* and on an interpretive display on the Tower Trail. The history of rock climbing at the tower has progressed steadily since the time of Weissner and Durance, with 27,000 climbers reaching the top by 1990.

The top of the Devils Tower supports a small prairie community. In 1992, researchers from the University of Wyoming identified twenty-one plant species including nine grasses, eight forbs, and four shrubs on the summit. Mice, wood rats, and chipmunks were also found.

Trails in the monument are well maintained with an easy-to-follow footway, but no blazes. No water is found along any of the trails. Bring a canteen and sun protection, as well as your camera. Deer are often seen along the trails. In summer, be prepared for sudden, often violent thunderstorms. Mountain bikes are not allowed on hiking trails in the monument.

For More Information: Contact Devils Tower National Monument, P.O. Box 8, Devils Tower, WY 82714, (307) 467-5501.

NORTH DAKOTA

White Butte

HIGHEST POINT IN NORTH DAKOTA

- ▲ **Description:** An easy hike to the highest point in North Dakota.
- ▲ **General Location:** Seven miles south of Amidon, North Dakota.
- ▲ **Access:** From Amidon, drive east 2 miles on U.S. 85. Then turn south and drive 6.5 miles south on a gravel road to the Buzalsky Ranch. Stop at the ranch and get permission to make the climb. White Butte is directly west.
- ▲ **Distance:** About 3 miles round trip.
- ▲ **Maps:** USGS Amidon, North Dakota, 7.5-minute quadrangle.

The highest point in North Dakota lies in the Chalky Buttes in the southwest part of the state. The buttes form a major divide between the Little Missouri River on the west, and Cedar Creek and the Cannonball River which drain east into the Missouri River. White Butte is close to U.S. 85, the road that connects the Black Hills to Theodore Roosevelt National Park, and can be easily climbed in half a day. The trip is especially popular with "highpointers," those who aspire to climb the high points of all fifty states.

There are no trails or established routes up White Butte. From the gravel road, hike west about one-half mile across a field. From the field, either climb due west to the top, or swing south and climb up the southeast ridge. There is a USGS marker and a register on top.

The Chalky Buttes are exceptionally pretty. To the south of White Butte, at the head of Sand Creek, are badlands that equal some of those found in Theodore Roosevelt National Park, or the Badlands Wilderness in Badlands National Park. To the west, across U.S. 85, is the Little Missouri National Grasslands and the Black Buttes.

White Butte lies on the southwest side of the Williston Basin, a major oil-producing region. In the center of the Williston Basin the bedrock is mostly Paleocene Sentinel Butte Formation. The Chalky Buttes are a

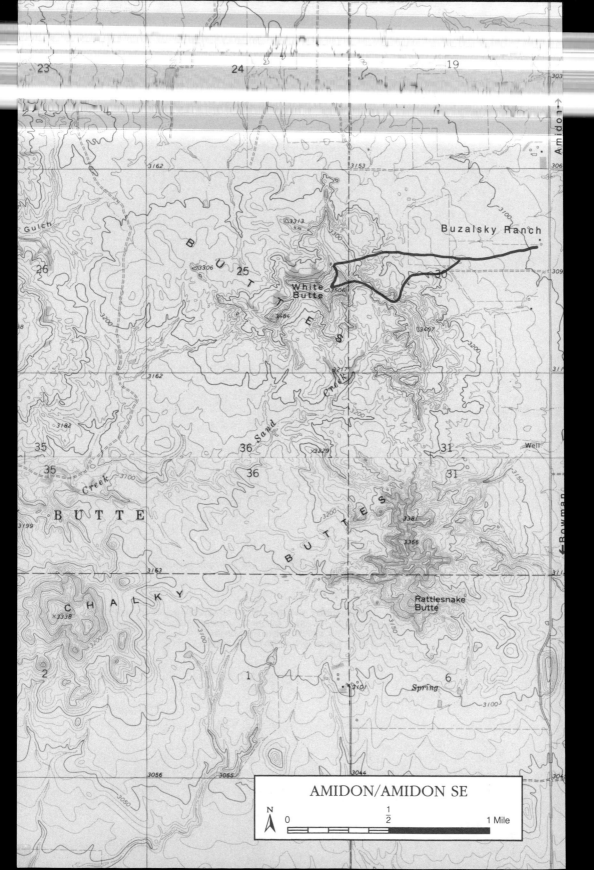

AMIDON/AMIDON SE

N

0   ½   1 Mile

relict island of younger Oligocene White River Group sedimentary rocks. The tops of White Butte, Radio Tower Butte, and Black Butte are capped by even younger Tertiary sedimentary rocks.

For many years a sign on U.S. 85 caused confusion about the location of White Butte. The sign seemed to point to a butte and radio tower only a mile east of the highway. At 3,472, the Radio Tower Butte is still one of the highest points in the state, but not the highest. The sign has been moved to a point east of Amidon so that it points to the correct butte. This confusion has caused several "highpointers," and a few North Dakota natives, to return to the Chalky Buttes to reach the correct summit.

White Butte and the surrounding land are on property owned by the Buzalsky family. Please respect their private property and ask at the ranch for permission to cross their land. If no one is at the ranch, permission to cross is not mandatory.

For More Information: See *Highpoints of the United States* by Don W. Holmes, or call the Buzalsky Ranch (701) 879-6306.

Petrified Forest Loop
THEODORE ROOSEVELT NATIONAL PARK

▲ **Description:** An overnight hike into the South Unit which includes an off-trail hike along the Little Missouri River.
▲ **General Location:** Three miles north of Medora, North Dakota.
▲ **Access:** Exit Interstate 94 at Medora and proceed to the park visitor center in Medora. From the visitor center follow the paved park road for 6.8 miles north to Peaceful Valley Ranch. Parking is available at the saddle horse concession.
▲ **Distance:** The loop is about twelve miles long.
▲ **Maps:** Theodore Roosevelt National Park Backcountry Guide; USGS Theodore Roosevelt National Park South Unit 1:24,000 Special Topographic Map.

Backcountry hiking is the best way to see Theodore Roosevelt National Park and the Little Missouri Badlands. The park has a beautiful, well-developed trail system that is perfect for easy weekend backpack trips. A loop on the west side of the South Unit combines two areas of special interest, the Petrified Forest Plateau and the bottom lands along the Little Missouri River.

From Peaceful Valley, negotiate a maze of paths leading down to the Little Missouri River. In high water, crossing the river may be the most difficult part of the trip, but even in May the river is usually less than knee deep. Once across, follow the Petrified Forest Loop Trail up the riverside bluffs onto Big Plateau.

Big Plateau is covered by a large prairie dog town that also attracts mule deer, coyotes, and bison. Beyond Big Plateau climb another bluff onto Petrified Forest Plateau. Along the base of this short climb the trail crosses a distinct geologic horizon which contains many of the fossil trees which give name to the plateau. Several weathered fossil stumps are visible from the trail. Remember that the National Park Service prohibits collecting fossil wood in the park in order to preserve the specimens that remain.

If you want to stay on trails, simply follow the Petrified Forest loop around to return to this point. Hiking across the east side of the plateau will convince even the most skeptical that North Dakota deserves its reputation for being flat.

If you want to complete a loop via the Little Missouri River, take the east fork at the head of Petrified Forest Plateau. The next mile and a half is almost perfectly level. The terrain is more varied beyond the point where the plateau narrows to form a gentle ridge which extends toward the north boundary of the park.

Leave the Petrified Forest Trail near the north boundary and hike northeast down a series of bluffs to the river bottom. A fine cluster of fossilized stumps sits nearby on a small bench just below the level of the trail. An easy descent route follows an abandoned jeep track along the nose of a small ridge before dropping into a small dry draw. Two groves of cottonwoods between the north boundary and VA well offer plenty of campsites.

A riverside camp has the advantage of water, otherwise unavailable in the backcountry. The wells found scattered throughout the park are water sources for wildlife and do not produce potable water. An added bonus is that the river which seemed so cold when you waded across in the morning may by afternoon be warm enough for swimming. The bluffs on either side of the river are perfect for wildlife watching or for photography.

On the second day follow the river downstream for five miles back to Peaceful Valley. Bluffs along the river can be climbed or bypassed by wading in the river. Pass through another huge prairie dog town at Beef Corral Bottom. Beyond the dog town, cross the river once more to avoid bushwhacking along the narrow strip between the river and the paved park road. End your hike at the parking area at Peaceful Valley.

The rocks in Theodore Roosevelt National Park were originally deposited as sediments during the Paleocene epoch. Rocks of the

Bullion Creek (also called Tongue River) and Sentinel Butte formations, which are both part of the Fort Union Group, are found. These sediments were deposited by the rivers and streams which drained the ancestral Rocky Mountains to the west. At this distance from the mountains the streams carried clay, silt, and sand, which are now the siltstone and sandstone beds of the Fort Union Group. As the ancestral Rocky Mountains began to rise a chain of volcanoes became active in what is now Montana and Wyoming. Huge eruptions of these volcanoes sent ash as far east as the Dakotas. These ash deposits are found in the park as beds of the clay mineral bentonite, commonly called gumbo. Bentonite has the remarkable ability to absorb five times its weight in water. Even more remarkable is how difficult bentonite is to walk on or drive over when wet. Gumbo is extremely sticky and slippery at the same time. There is no cure, only prevention; it is best to stay out of the badlands after a recent rain.

Petrified wood is common throughout Theodore Roosevelt National Park. The rapid rate of Paleocene sedimentation accounts for the formation of fossil wood. The Paleocene climate was subtropical, and much of the landscape was covered by thick forests and swamps. Rapid changes in stream channels, or volcanic eruptions, caused many trees to be buried before they had a chance to decay. Following further burial, groundwater began to circulate through the sediments. Silica dissolved from the ash beds was redeposited in wood as ground water saturated the buried trees. Eventually silica replaced and coated much of the woody plant tissues to create petrified wood. The most common type of petrified wood in the park is preserved tree stumps.

Spring and fall are the best times to visit the Little Missouri Badlands. The change of seasons moderates the temperature extremes characteristic of the northern plains. Trails are well marked and easy to follow. The huge posts which mark the trails across the prairie are testaments both to longing of bison for good scratching posts and the perseverance of park rangers in marking trails.

At any time of year carry plenty of water since none is found along the trails. No open fires are allowed in the backcountry, and mountain bikes are also prohibited. Overnight trips require a free backcountry permit which may be picked up at the Medora Visitor Center between 8:00 and 4:30. There are no established backcountry campsites.

For More Information: Contact Theodore Roosevelt National Park, P.O. Box 7, Medora, ND 58645, (701) 623-4466.

Jones–Lower Paddock Creek Trails Loop

THEODORE ROOSEVELT NATIONAL PARK

▲ **Description:** A rugged circuit through the center of the South Unit for hikers or horses.

▲ **General Location:** Five miles northeast of Medora, North Dakota.

▲ **Access:** From the visitor center at Medora, drive north on the paved park road for 8.4 miles to the parking area at the Jones Creek Trailhead. If your group has more than one vehicle, leave one at the Paddock Creek Trailhead near the Halliday Well Group Campsite to avoid one mile of hiking along the park road.

▲ **Distance:** The loop is 11.8 miles around.

▲ **Maps:** Theodore Roosevelt National Park Backcountry Guide; USGS Theodore Roosevelt National Park South Unit 1;24,000 Special Topographic Map.

One of the most popular trips in Theodore Roosevelt National Park is a loop which connects the trails along Jones and Paddock creeks. This loop can be hiked or ridden in one long day, or combined with the upper Paddock Creek and Talkington trails to make an overnight trip. This hike through quiet creek bottoms leads through country much rougher than other trails in the South Unit.

Begin by hiking east on the Jones Creek Trail, crossing the main fork of Jones Creek twice. As the trail winds along the creek bottom through green ash and grasses, notice how clusters of juniper are found only on the shaded and moister north-facing slopes. At the first trail junction at 2.6 miles, turn south to follow the lower Talkington Trail for 2 miles. Climb over a butte which marks the divide between Jones and Paddock creeks. Then descend to a prominent tributary of Paddock Creek, where a connector trail branches south from the Talkington Trail.

Follow the connector trail south for 1.8 miles down the tributary. Along the way pass areas where erosion of sandstone in the Bullion Creek formation has produced steep sand dunes. The last one-half mile of the connector trail is adjacent to the park loop road. Reach Paddock Creek and a small turnout from the road which marks the Paddock Creek Trail.

Follow the Lower Paddock Creek Trail downstream and west for 3.9 miles, keeping in the main valley. Notice how the meanders in Paddock Creek are tighter and more closely spaced than those in the Little Missouri River. The rate of water flow in a stream, the gradient of the stream, and other properties of a watershed are related to the size of the stream. Streams cut meanders as a means to dissipate the potential energy of water which is created by the difference in elevation of the water in the stream and the elevation of the area the stream discharges into. Subsidiary streams, such as Paddock Creek, have high potential energy which is spent on cutting more meanders, while main streams, such as the Little Missouri River, have less potential energy and therefore more gentle meanders. The high level of erosion in subsidiary streams means that the bed of the stream is rougher and the flow turbulent. Despite appearances, water in a turbulent, subsidiary stream flows at a slower rate than water in a larger, smooth-flowing river.

The Lower Paddock Creek Trail passes through a remarkably large prairie dog town. Bison often graze near the head of the dog town. The town fills the entire valley floor as you approach the Halliday Well Group Campground. If you were unable to leave a car at the Paddock Creek Trailhead near the campground, you must walk 0.5 mile west to the park loop road, and then one mile north along the road to the Jones Creek Trailhead. You may walk along the road, or follow a maze of trails created by the park's horse concessionaire on the west side of the road.

Since the loop starts near the stables at Peaceful Valley, it is equally suitable for hikers or horses. Either way, keep an eye out for wildlife. You're likely to see wild turkeys, mule deer, bison, or coyotes in addition to the prairie dogs near Halliday Well.

Jones Creek was one of the first trails in Theodore Roosevelt National Park to be marked with carsonite posts and is especially easy to follow. The Paddock Creek Trail is not shown on older park topographic maps.

For More Information: Contact Theodore Roosevelt National Park, P.O. Box 7, Medora, ND 58645, (701) 623-4466.

Caprock–Coulee Trail
THEODORE ROOSEVELT NATIONAL PARK

▲ **Description:** The first three-quarter mile of this loop is a self-guiding nature trail.
▲ **General Location:** Thirteen miles south of Watford City, North Dakota.
▲ **Access:** From U.S. 85, drive 6.5 miles west on the paved park road to a parking area on the north side of the road.
▲ **Distance:** The loop is 4.3 miles around.
▲ **Maps:** Theodore Roosevelt National Park Backcountry Guide; USGS Theodore Roosevelt National Park North Unit 1:24,000 Special Topographic Map.

If you have time for only one hike in the North Unit of Theodore Roosevelt National Park, it should be the Caprock–Coulee Nature Trail. The first three-quarter mile of this trail is a self-guiding introduction to

THEODORE ROOSEVELT
NATIONAL MEMORIAL PARK
(NORTH UNIT)

N

0   ½   1 Mile

the geology and botany of the badlands and prairie. Beyond the self-guiding portion, lies some of the best ridge-line walking found in the park. This trail is closed to horses.

Follow the numbered posts north from the trailhead along Caprock–Coulee. At the end of the self-guided trail, turn west, then south, to climb through a grove of juniper and green ash. Western wheatgrass is the dominant grass in these groves. The trail turns west again at the top of a narrow ridge. Follow the ridge west as it widens into open prairie before reaching the paved park road 2.7 miles from the start.

Follow alongside the park road for 0.2 mile south to Riverbend Overlook, where a side trail leads south to a stone shelter. The trail stays on the roadside and crosses the heads of two small coulees. Then turn right off the road onto the crest of a ridge leading east. Reach a junction with the Achenbach Trail 0.6 mile from Riverbend Overlook and continue east. Cross two small saddles offering spectacular views over the Little Missouri River, before turning north off of the ridge. Descend steadily to the trailhead, which is 0.8 mile from the Achenbach junction.

The diversity of the Caprock–Coulee Nature Trail makes it an ideal introduction to Theodore Roosevelt National Park. The trail crosses most of the park's major habitats: narrow coulees, juniper groves, badlands ridges, and open prairie. The views are superb, particularly on the south side where the trail overlooks the Little Missouri River.

Coyotes, mule deer, and rabbits find the trail easy going, and you may also see tracks from one of the park's rare bobcats.

The display of geologic features along the trail is impressive. On the self-guided portion you'll learn how water cuts the soft bedrock and creates badlands. You will see examples of lignite seams, beds of bentonite, landslides, slump blocks, and caprocks.

A few bison trails intersect the Caprock–Coulee Trail north of the park road, but the park is in the process of adding new carsonite posts to mark trails. There is no water on the trail, and you'll probably need some after being exposed to North Dakota's special combination of sun and wind.

The park road is open as far as the Caprock–Coulee Trailhead in winter. Squaw Creek Campground is open in winter, but there is no water. This is a good time to study the abundant animal tracks in the snow.

For More Information: Contact Theodore Roosevelt National Park, P.O. Box 7, Medora, ND 58645, (701) 623-4466, or call the North Unit at (701) 842-2333.

Achenbach Trail Loop

THEODORE ROOSEVELT NATIONAL PARK

▲ **Description:** A multiday loop through the North Unit for hikers and horses.
▲ **General Location:** Fourteen miles south of Watford City, North Dakota.
▲ **Access:** From U.S. 85, drive 4.9 miles west on the paved park scenic drive. Turn south onto the road to Squaw Creek Campground. The Achenbach Trail starts across the river from the campground.
▲ **Distance:** Use parts of the Caprock–Coulee and Buckhorn trails to form a 17.6-mile loop.
▲ **Maps:** Theodore Roosevelt National Park Backcountry Guide; USGS Theodore Roosevelt National Park North Unit 1:24,000 Special Topographic Map.

The Achenbach Trail explores some of the roughest terrain found in Theodore Roosevelt National Park. In the park's North Unit, relief is greater and the terrain more rugged than in the South Unit. Except for a narrow corridor around the park scenic drive, most of the North Unit is designated wilderness. Through the heart of this country is a loop that is long enough for a two- or three-day trip.

From the Squaw Creek Campground, hike 0.2 mile to the Little Missouri River. Cross the river, and then the floodplain, before climbing through a mixture of badlands and juniper groves. Once onto the prairie above the river, follow a new trail west and then south to a point near the park boundary. Continue west on a north-facing slope to reach a junction with a road that leads south. Then enter the Achenbach Hills and reach a junction with a faint trail leading north to Achenbach Spring. This trail junction is 4.5 miles from the Little Missouri River.

Continue along the north side of the Achenbach Hills through open prairie. Descend gradually to reach the Little Missouri River 2.2 miles beyond the Achenbach Spring junction. Take special care to follow the trail along the river bottom and across the river. Hike about one mile north along the west side of the river before climbing steadily up to Sperati Point. Once out of the valley, and onto the prairie, continue north to a junction with an old dirt road. Then hike north through the prairie for one-half mile before turning east to reach Oxbow Overlook 3.7 miles past the river crossing.

From the overlook, descend steadily back down to the river bottom. The North Achenbach Trail follows the north edge of the river bottom to the crossing of Appel Creek. From Appel Creek climb gradually east, then steadily north to reach a junction with the Caprock–Coulee Trail 4.2 miles from Oxbow Overlook.

To return to Squaw Creek Campground, follow the Caprock–Coulee Trail for 0.8 mile to the scenic drive and the trailhead. Then follow the Buckhorn Trail 2 miles back to the campground. An alternate route for hikers only begins one-half mile beyond the Achenbach Trail junction where the Caprock–Coulee Trail turns north. Hikers can continue southeast on the ridge crest until the ridge ends at the river bottom about one-quarter mile north of Squaw Creek Campground. The self-guiding Squaw Creek Nature Trail also begins from the campground.

In hot weather the closeness of the river is a luxury for most travellers. Neither river crossing is difficult. The water is usually less than knee deep although it can be much higher. The warm, silty water isn't ideal for a midday swim, but you can cool off by wallowing in some of the deeper pools. Channel catfish, goldeye shiners, and flathead chub live in the river within the park.

As with any hike in the badlands you may confuse your trail with those made by bison. Carry a compass and topographic map and know how to use them. This is a good area to watch wildlife, particularly wild turkeys, but you may also encounter ticks, prairie rattlesnakes, and poison ivy. There is no drinking water along the loop, so carry your own. If you must drink from the silty Little Missouri River, filter the water with a unit designed to remove giardia bacteria. To save wear on your filter and pump, prefilter with a double-layer coffee filter, or let the water settle overnight.

Backcountry regulations are the same as in the South Unit. Horse groups and hikers planning to camp overnight must obtain a free backcountry use permit in person. Open fires are prohibited and you must practice no trace camping.

Theodore Roosevelt arrived in the Dakotas in 1883. This was the era of open range, when cattle grazed without fences. Roosevelt's Maltese Cross Ranch was located south of Medora, but he preferred life on his isolated Elkhorn Ranch. Unfortunately for ranchers the cattle boom was short lived. The harsh winter of 1886–87 killed large numbers of stock and the subsequent summers were much drier.

The park is home to a small herd of Texas longhorn cattle. The longhorns serve as a living reminder of the cattle boom that occurred during Roosevelt's time. You probably won't see the longhorns along the trail, they generally stay on the river bottom east of Squaw Creek Campground.

This short period profoundly influenced Theodore Roosevelt. His writings are filled with an appreciation for the quiet simplicity of ranch life and the beauty of the natural world. He saw the near extinction of bison, and he emerged from this experience as a powerful force in

American conservation. The solitude and beauty found today in the North Unit is a fitting tribute to the president who most strongly shaped our park system and conservation ethic.

For More Information: Contact Theodore Roosevelt National Park, P.O. Box 7, Medora, ND 58645, (701) 623-4466, or call the North Unit at (701) 842-2333.

Indian–Travois Trails Loop
LITTLE MISSOURI STATE PARK

▲ **Description:** A hike from the prairie to the Little Missouri River for hikers and horses.
▲ **General Location:** Twenty-one miles northeast of Killdeer, North Dakota.
▲ **Access:** From Killdeer, drive 19 miles north on North Dakota 22. Turn east onto the gravel park road and stay left at the next two intersections. Drive 2.2 miles to the trailhead, which is located by a group of picnic shelters and horse corrals.
▲ **Distance:** The loop is 4½ miles around.
▲ **Maps:** USGS Mandavee SW, North Dakota, 7.5-minute quadrangle.

Little Missouri State Park is the hidden gem of the North Dakota badlands. A beautiful network of trails is concealed in the park's 5,748 acres. The park is maintained for visitors seeking primitive camping and little-developed hiking and horseback trails. A loop combining the Travois and Indian trails is the quickest route to descend from the grassland bluffs to the Little Missouri River 500 feet below.

Both trails leave from the north picnic area at a gate near the northmost horse corral. The Indian Trail descends from the bluffs through a grove of junipers, then enters badlands. Climb up a ridge, then pass a collapsed fence. Stay right at the junction with the Hogback Trail. At 1.5 miles, just before another fence, reach the junction with the Travois Trail.

Turn north onto the Travois Trail and descend steadily on an old road toward the Little Missouri River. The descent begins steeply through juniper, then becomes more gradual. Watch carefully for thin black lignite seams, and thick bands of gray bentonite clay. The Hogback Trail intersects the Travois just before reaching the junction with the TX Trail near a stock tank. To reach the river, hike due north from this intersection.

To finish the loop, turn southwest and begin to climb back toward the bluffs. The trail follows an old roadway the entire distance, but may become confused with other roads and cattle trails. You will cross one standing fence and follow a draw on the opposite side of a stock tank with a flowing well. Near the prairie rim, the Travois Trail turns abruptly southeast before reaching the trailhead three miles from the Indian Trail junction.

The Little Missouri State Park Map lists ten trails with a total length of twenty-eight miles. However, park personnel report that there is little interest from hikers in the established trails because the terrain is so open and navigation so easy. Most groups simply follow the main canyons or ridges down to the river. Horses are restricted to designated trails. Trail markings are limited to short posts located at trail intersections.

Most park users are on horseback. Spruce Hill Ranch, located at the junction of the park road and North Dakota 22, offers trail rides to the public. Corrals are available at the trailhead for those who bring their own horses. Hikers are welcome on the trails, and can often reach places inaccessible to horses.

Few restrictions apply in Little Missouri State Park. No backcountry permits are necessary. No trace camping is required in the backcountry. Water can be obtained only at the trailhead campground and fires are restricted to the campground. Camping permits are $5 per day and $1 per day for horses. A ranger is stationed at the park from Memorial Day to Labor Day, otherwise self-registration is available.

Besides the solitude of a primitive park, visitors come for the wildlife watching. Coyotes, mule deer, eagles, badgers, and prairie dogs are found along with prairie rattlesnakes.

The park feels much bigger than it really is. The 5,748 acres of the park does not include the river bottom, which is controlled by the Army Corps of Engineers, or some private land which is crossed by the trails.

For More Information: Contact Park Manager, Lake Sakakawea State Park, Riverdale, ND 58565, (701) 487-3315.

Appendix A

HIGHPOINTS
OF THE BLACK HILLS

For many people an ideal hike ends on a tall, scenic mountaintop. Unfortunately, for any number of reasons, it is hard to find this ideal in the Black Hills. There are only a handful of distinctive peaks in the hills, and few of these are among the tallest peaks. Years of road building in the hills have established road access to many of the highest points. Among the few exceptions, only some of these have trail access. Once these few summits have been reached, finding other Black Hills peaks to climb on foot can be a challenge.

Finding an interesting climb in the Black Hills requires substantial searching through USGS and BHNF maps to find a peak, a route, and public access to both. The few good climbs that result from this search (Sylvan Peak, Silver Peak, Spearfish Peak, and Pillar Peak) compensate for some other poor routes.

The list developed below required making, and bending, a few rules. First, the list is not strictly by elevation. Many points on the Limestone Plateau between Bear Mountain and Crook's Tower rise above 7,000 feet above sea level, but the plateau offers few summits worthy of ascent. Secondly, the peak must be a point of interest geologically, historically, or otherwise. Finally, there must be a reasonable nonmotorized route to the summit.

At just half the elevation of the giants in nearby Colorado, the 7,000-foot summits of the Black Hills form an even more select group. With the exception of Harney and Sylvan peaks, all the 7,000-footers have access roads that can be driven or easily ridden on a mountain bike.

Black Hills National Forest fire lookouts are another group of peaks with interesting views. These summits will all have currently maintained access roads, though alternative routes to many can be found. Abandoned and dismantled fire lookouts can be found by searching USGS quadrangles and previous editions of the Black Hills National Forest map. Without the added advantage of the tower, some, such as Cicero Peak, have no view at all. The access roads to the abandoned towers usually are fun rides on a mountain bike.

In addition to Harney Peak, a few other interesting peaks have access only by trail. These few routes are all described in this guide.

The final group of summits is a Wish List. Inyan Kara Mountain, Sundance Mountain, and the Missouri Buttes are all on private land, or access to them is completely restricted by private land. Through careful research, and a tactful approach, some may be climbed by obtaining permission of the landowners involved. Unfortunately, all three are still off limits to the public.

Mountain bikes are ideal for exploring Black Hills summits, especially the 7,000-footers and those with lookout towers. *A Mountain Bikers Guide to the Black Hills of South Dakota and Wyoming* contains mountain bike routes to many of these summits. Summits in the northern Black Hills can often be reached on skis in winter. Many of the summits are also excellent for trail runs. See "Appendix B" for more information on trail runs.

The list developed below is highly subjective and reflects personal experience much more than elevation. Technical climbs, such as Devils Tower or the Cathedral Spires, are beyond the scope of this guide. Emphasis has been placed on trips at least one-half-day long or with at least 1,000 feet of vertical gain. The major geologic divisions of the Black Hills are represented: Terry Peak in the Tertiary intrusive igneous rocks in the north, Battle Mountain in the Dakota Hogback, Crook's Tower on the Limestone Plateau, Harney Peak in the Harney Peak Granite, Scruton Mountain in the Precambrian metasedimentary rocks, and Bear Mountain in the Archean granite-gneiss terrain.

Whether or not the Black Hills needs its own equivalent of Colorado's "fourteeners" or the Adirondack "forty-six," these summits should provide enough goals for those who need or want them. Many of the mountains listed are not described in this guide. For those peaks, the section, township, and range data are listed. The Black Hills National Forest map shows all the peaks listed except Mount Warner, Sylvan Peak, and Missouri Buttes.

ELEV.	NAME (tower), USGS Quad, (section, township, range)
7,242	Harney Peak (tower), Custer, SD
7,200	Odakota Mountain, Ditch Creek, SD
7,166	Bear Mountain (tower), Berne, SD
7,164	Green Mountain, Ditch Creek, SD (S21, T1S, R2E)
7,137	Crooks Tower, Crooks Tower, SD (S6, T2N, R2E)
7,064	Terry Peak (tower), Lead, SD (S11, T4N, R2E)
7,048	Crows Nest Peak (tower removed), Crows Nest Peak, SD (S11, T1N, R1E)
7,000	"Sylvan Peak," Custer, SD
6,937	Flag Mountain (tower removed), Deerfield, SD (S1, T1N, R2E)
6,890	Little Devils Tower, Custer, SD
6,804	Custer Peak (tower), Minnesota Ridge, SD
6,650	Warren Peak (tower), Sundance West, WY (S20, T52N, R63W)
6,623	Cement Ridge (tower), Old Baldy Mountain, WY-SD (S5, T50N, R60W)
6,483	Signal Hill (tower removed), Signal Hill, SD (S2, T3S, R2E)
6,468	St. Elmo Peak, Custer, SD (S13, T2S, R4E)
6,368	Inyan Kara Mountain, Inyan Kara Mountain, WY (S19, T49N, R62W)
6,358	Castle Peak, Rochford, SD (S35, T2N, R3E)
6,166	Cicero Peak (tower removed), Cicero Peak, SD (S29, T4S, R5E)
6,096	Old Baldy Mountain, Old Baldy Mountain WY-SD
6,096	Summit Ridge (tower), Fanny Peak, WY-SD (S19, T2S, R1E)
6,023	Mount Coolidge (tower), Mount Coolidge, SD (S35, T3S, R5E)
5,922	Scruton Mountain (tower), Silver City, SD (S16, T1N, R5E)
5,889	Mount Warner, Mount Rushmore, SD
5,824	Sundance Mountain (tower), Sundance West, WY (S24, T51N, R63W)
5,810	Silver Peak, Silver City, SD
5,800	Spearfish Peak, Spearfish, SD
5,760	Crow Peak, Maurice, SD
5,676	Mount Theodore Roosevelt (tower), Spearfish, SD (S16, T5N, R3E)
5,662	Elk Mountain (tower), Clifton, WY-SD (S7, T4S, R1E)
5,469	Pillar Peak, Deadwood South, SD
5,374	Missouri Buttes, Missouri Buttes, WY (S33, T45N, R66W)
5,333	Veterans Peak (tower), Deadman Mountain, SD (S5, T4N, R5E)
5,331	Boulder Hill (tower), Mount Rushmore, SD
5,112	Devils tower, Devils tower, WY (S7, T53N, R65W)
5,013	Rankin Ridge (tower), Mount Coolidge, SD
4,848	Parker Peak (tower removed), Minnekahta, SD (S31, T7S, R4E)
4,788	Pilger Mountain (tower removed), Jewel Cave SW, SD (S29, T6S, R2E)
4,434	Battle Mountain (tower), Hot Springs, SD (S18, T7S, R6E)
4,426	Bear Butte, Fort Meade, SD

TRAIL RUNNING
IN THE BLACK HILLS

The sport of trail running is a hybrid of hiking and distance running. An excellent aerobic workout, trail running also provides the solitude and escape normally associated with a leisurely hiking trip. In the Black Hills, runners can use maintained hiking trails, little-used dirt roads, or the access roads to fire towers and lookouts.

Trail running builds strength, endurance, and aerobic capacity. These workouts do little to improve speed or quickness, although running on steep hills or rocky trails can improve agility. Trail runs are more difficult than ordinary distance runs. This is not a sport for someone beginning an exercise program, a solid running base is required. The sport is best suited to distance runners, or hikers and backpackers who want to improve their fitness. Trail runs are also excellent training for local Black Hills races such as Mystic Mountain, Elk Mountain, or the Centennial Trail Ultra 50.

Done correctly, trail running provides the opportunity for midweek explorations that can free your weekends for more ambitious projects. Most of the hiking trails in the Black Hills are designed for day hikes, and most can be done as afternoon runs. My preference is to seek out routes that end on mountain tops, preferably those with good views. Fire towers, lookouts, and summits with hiking trails generally make the best routes.

Trail running requires more preparation than normal training runs. Carry water, and a little food, in a fanny pack with a water bottle holder. The running packs made by Ultimate Direction are some of the best fanny packs around. If unfamiliar with a route it is a good idea to carry a copy of the map of the area in a ziplock bag. In spring, beware of afternoon electrical storms and be prepared to retreat from exposed areas if a storm strikes. Plan on a slow, steady pace. Most of the runs described below can be done without walking. It is not unusual to go slower than a ten-minute mile pace on long or steep hills, you'll be able to make up the time on the descent.

Bear Butte: 3.5 miles round trip and 975 feet of ascent. Bear Butte State Park is located 2.5 miles north of Sturgis on U.S. 79. This is the shortest of the mountain runs and the best for beginners. Follow the Summit Trail, which is also the last one and three-quarters mile of the Centennial Trail, unrelentingly to the top. To make a loop on the way down, follow the Ceremonial Trail back to the parking area. This is a very scenic course; if you don't like this route you probably won't enjoy trail running.

Mount Theodore Roosevelt: 7 miles round trip and 1,080 feet of ascent. This is the standard hill workout for runners in the Lead–Deadwood area. Start at the junction of Main and Denver streets in Deadwood, or as close as you can park. Denver Street soon becomes a gravel BHNF road. Follow the gravel road to a picnic area then follow a short hiking trail to the tower on top. The last mile of the course is relatively flat, but the climb is a killer.

Crow Peak: My personal favorite. The trail climbs 1,600 feet in 3.5 grueling miles. The Crow Peak Trail starts 4 miles south of Spearfish on the Higgins Gulch Road. The trail becomes increasingly steeper and rockier toward the top. Your reward for the climb is a beautiful view of Spearfish and the northern Black Hills.

Old Baldy: The trailhead is located 1.2 miles north of BHNF Road 222 on BHNF Road 134. This 6.5-mile loop actually loses elevation between the trailhead and the summit of Old Baldy. This is a great run over rolling terrain with good views. Only the last half mile of the climb up the cone of Old Baldy is steep.

Terry Peak: There are two sane routes for this peak. The Terry Peak Summit Road leads 3.3 miles and 880 feet from U.S. 85 to the lookout tower. A short, steep option is to follow a maintenance road from the base of the Blue Chairlift 1,100 lung-searing feet to the top. Runners suffering from the long term effects of oxygen deprivation might consider following the old route of the Deadwood Trail Ultra 50 course from Miller Creek at Centennial Prairie, 18 miles and 2,900 feet of pure aerobic intensity.

Custer Peak: Another peak with multiple routes. The simplest is to start at the junction of U.S. 385 and BHNF Road 216 and follow Road 216 to the junction with the summit road, which is located on the saddle at the west shoulder of Custer Peak. The summit road spirals around the cone of Custer Peak to the top. This is a ten-mile round trip and includes 1,300 feet of ascent. The saddle can also be reached either from U.S. 385 or the Rochford Road by Snowmobile Trail 7.

Veteran's Peak: 4 miles round trip and 870 feet vertical. From the junction of BHNF Roads 170 and 135, follow Road 135 south to a dirt road heading east which leads to the radio towers on top. Veteran's Peak offers good views of the ski runs on Terry Peak and Deer Mountain.

Scruton Mountain (Seth Bullock Lookout). From the junction of U.S. 385 and BHNF Road 251 follow Road 251 to BHNF Road 156. Turn right onto Road 156, cross a gate barring vehicle traffic and grunt up a series of switchbacks to the lookout tower on top. Nine hundred and twenty feet of climbing are packed into this six-mile round trip.

Harney Peak: If you want to avoid the crowds on the route from Sylvan Lake, try the north side. From the Willow Creek Trailhead it is five miles and 2,200 feet to the top, plenty of time to learn more than you'll ever want to know about controlling your pace.

Cement Ridge: A five-mile round trip with 400 feet of climbing. Drive west of Savoy to the north junction of BHNF Roads 134 and 222. Follow Road 222 for 3 miles to a junction with BHNF Road 103 and Snowmobile Trail 3. Run up BHNF Road 103 which becomes BHNF Road 867 in Wyoming, and follow Road 867 up the southeast ridge to the tower on top of Cement Ridge. This is a great fall run when the aspen leaves have turned on the Limestone Plateau.

Many other peaks in the Black Hill are used for trail runs or have good potential. Battle Mountain near Hot Springs, Warren Peak near Sundance, Bear Mountain, Crook's Tower, Pillar Peak, and Whitetail Peak near Rochford are just a few. Other trails which are fun to run include the Centennial Trail, the new Deerfield Lake loop, and the trail systems around Harney Peak and in Wind Cave National Park.

Appendix C
CENTENNIAL TRAIL MILEAGE SUMMARY

The Centennial Trail is the only long trail in the Black Hills and Badlands region. As it traverses the length of the hills, the trail becomes the responsibility of a variety of government agencies. The regulations that apply to the trail vary according to the administrative agency and are summarized in the *Centennial Trail User's Guide*. The allowed uses of the trail will be of the most concern to the users of this guide. Mountain bikes are prohibited on the trail in the Black Elk Wilderness, Wind Cave National Park, and the northern part of Bear Butte State Park. Conversely, motorized vehicles are allowed on the trail between Pilot Knob and Dalton Lake.

As regulations vary between agencies, so do standards of trail marking and maintenance. Much of the Centennial Trail is scheduled for improvement in the next few years, but it is unlikely that these improvements will upgrade the entire trail to standards desired by trail users and administrators. Government agencies can be surprisingly responsive to comments about trail use. If you see a problem, don't hesitate to report it. Be specific, note exactly where an unmarked trail junction is located, or report exactly where motorized vehicles access a trail that they are not permitted on. Just be sure to be equally diligent about reporting the positive aspects of your trip.

You can also help by doing some routine maintenance on your trip. Simple things, such as cleaning out water bars, restanding fallen signs, picking up litter, or throwing a few rocks out of the trail help to make the trail a lot nicer for those who follow you.

	CUMULATIVE MILEAGE	DISTANCE
Norbeck Dam Trailhead	0.0	0.0
Leave Beaver Creek	2.0	2.0
WCNP Trail 5	4.5	2.5
NPS Road 5	6.0	1.5
CSP Road 7	9.5	3.5
Wildlife Loop Road	13.5	4.0
CSP Road 4	15.0	1.5
French Creek Trailhead	15.5	0.5
Bypass Trail South	17.0	1.5
Bypass Trail North	18.3	1.3
U.S. 16A	20.3	2.0
South Dakota 87	26.3	6.0
Iron Creek Trailhead	27.0	0.8
CT/15 Junction	28.3	1.3
CT/16 Junction	29.0	0.7
Enter Wilderness	30.1	1.1
CT/5 Junction South	31.1	1.0
CT/14 Junction	32.8	1.7
Leave Wilderness	34.3	1.5
CT/5 Junction North	34.6	0.3
Big Pine Trailhead/SD 244	35.2	0.6
BHNF Road 353	35.7	0.5
Samelius Trailhead	38.7	3.0
BHNF Road 531	39.3	0.6
Mount Warner	42.0	2.7
BHNF Road 392	45.2	3.2
Sheridan Dam	46.9	1.7
North End Bypass	47.9	1.0
Dakota Point Trailhead	48.2	0.3
Sheridan Lake Road	48.9	0.7
BHNF Road 551	50.2	1.3
BHNF Road 160	51.7	1.5
North End Bald Hills	53.0	1.3
Brush Creek Trailhead/772	54.6	1.6
Exit Gold Standard	57.8	3.2
Tamarack Trailhead	59.1	1.3
Rapid Creek Trailhead	59.7	0.6
U.S. 385	61.0	1.3

(continued)

	CUMULATIVE MILEAGE	DISTANCE
BHNF Road 264	61.5	0.5
Smoker Gulch	63.5	2.0
Deer Creek Trailhead	64.5	1.0
U.S. 385	66.4	1.9
Pilot Knob Trailhead/		
BHNF Road 208	67.8	1.4
BHNF Road 152	69.5	1.7
BHNF Road 740	71.1	1.6
Boxelder Canyon	73.0	1.9
Boxelder Forks Trailhead	74.2	1.2
Boxelder Campground	74.7	0.5
BHNF Road 140	76.4	1.7
BHNF Road 678	77.6	1.2
Nemo Road	78.4	0.8
Contour Road-East	81.1	2.7
Dalton Lake/BHNF Road 224	83.2	2.1
BHNF Road 704-South	84.2	1.0
BHNF Road 704-North	86.3	2.1
BHNF Road 702	87.3	1.0
Elk Creek-East End	87.9	0.6
Bypass-North	89.4	1.5
Elk Creek Trailhead/		
BHNF Road 168	91.2	1.8
BHNF Road 169	91.9	0.7
BHNF Road 139-South End	94.0	2.1
Point 5,045	95.0	1.0
Bulldog Gulch-East End	97.9	2.9
BHNF Road 139-North	98.4	0.5
BLM/BHNF Boundary	100.5	2.1
I-90	101.1	0.6
Alkali Creek Trailhead	101.6	0.5
Fort Meade Road	104.0	2.4
Fort Meade Trailhead	106.5	2.5
BLM/BBSP Boundary	110.7	4.2
Bear Butte Lake Trailhead	111.9	1.2
Bear Butte Trailhead	113.3	1.4
Bear Butte Summit	114.9	1.6

Hikers will require one week or more for the entire trail. For persons attempting to hike the entire Centennial Trail in a single trip, their greatest obstacle will be getting water. Few trailheads have drinking water supplies and there are only a few streams along the trail that flow year-round. Water from streams and lakes should be treated before drinking. In addition to the Black Hills National Forest campgrounds described in the guide, there are several private campgrounds with small stores located along U.S. 385. Supplies are also available in Custer, Hill City, and Lead–Deadwood.

For mountain bike riders or horseback riders water problems are less serious, since they can travel farther per day than hikers. Most mountain bikers can ride the trail in three to four long days.

One possible ten-day itinerary for the entire Centennial Trail is listed below. Keep in mind that the campgrounds at Sheridan and Pactola lakes are often full during summer weekends. Mileages shown for these two campgrounds do not include the extra distance between the Centennial Trail and the campground. At some of these sites you may want to do your cooking and fill up with water before moving on to a quieter campsite.

Day 1	15.0	15.0	French Creek Horse Camp (first water)
Day 2	12.0	27.0	Iron Creek Horse Camp
Day 3	8.2	35.2	Horsethief Lake (longer via Harney Peak)
Day 4	11.8	46.0	Calumet Trailhead (Sheridan Southside CG)
Day 5	13.7	59.7	Rapid Creek Trailhead (Pactola CG)
Day 6	15.0	74.7	Boxelder Campground
Day 7	8.5	83.2	Dalton Lake Campground
Day 8	6.2	89.4	Elk Creek (camp along creek)
Day 9	12.2	101.6	Alkali Creek Campground
Day 10	14.9	116.5	Finish (includes descent of Bear Butte)

Appendix D
SELECTED BIBLIOGRAPHY

Conn, Herb and Jan. *The Jewel Cave Adventure*. Cave Books, 1977.

Dewitt, Ed, J. A. Redden, Anna Burrack Wilson, David Buscher, and John S. Dersch. *Mineral Resource Potential and Geology of the Black Hills National Forest: South Dakota and Wyoming*. USGS Bulletin 1580, 1986.

Fielder, Mildred. *Hiking Trails of the Black Hills*. North Plains Press, 1973.

Fielder, Mildred. *A Guide to Black Hills Ghost Mines*. North Plains Press, 1972.

Froiland, Sven G. *Natural History of the Black Hills and Badlands*. The Center for Western Studies, 1990.

Gardiner, S. and D. Guilmette. *Devils Tower National Monument: A Climber's Guide*. The Mountaineers Books.

Holmes, Don W. *Highpoints of the United States*. Cordillera Press, 1990.

Horning, D. and H. Marriot. *A Mountain Bikers Guide to the Black Hills: South Dakota and Wyoming*. Poorperson's Guidebooks, 1987.

Kaye, B. and H. Schoch. *Theodore Roosevelt: The Story Behind the Scenery*. H. C. Publications, 1993.

Keve Hauk, Joy. *Badlands: Its Life and Landscape*. Badlands Natural History Association, 1969.

McGee, Dingus and the Last Pioneer Woman. *Black Hills Needles: Selected Free Climbs*. Poorperson's Guidebooks, 1981.

McGee, Dingus and the Last Pioneer Woman. *Free Climbs of Devils Tower*, 1990.

Melius, Michael. *True*. Tensleep Publications, 1991.

Parker, Watson. *Gold in the Black Hills*. University of Nebraska Press, 1966.

Patterson, Colin J. and Alvis L. Lisenbee, editors. *Metallogeny of Gold in the Black Hills, South Dakota*. Society of Economic Geologists Guidebook Series Volume 7, 1990.

Piana, Paul. *Touch the Sky*. The American Alpine Club, 1983.

Raymond, W.H. and R.U. King. *Geologic Map of the Badlands National Monument and Vicinity: West-Central South Dakota*. USGS MI Map I-934, 1978.

Robinson, Charles S. *Geology of Devils Tower National Monument, Wyoming*. USGS, 1985.

Tabori, Stewart and Chang. *Guide to the National Parks: Rocky Mountains and Great Plains*. Sierra Club, 1984.

INDEX

TRIP NOTES

TRIP NOTES

TRIP NOTES

TRIP NOTES

TRIP NOTES

Other Cordillera Guidebooks From
JOHNSON BOOKS

ARIZONA'S MOUNTAINS
A Hiking Guide to the Grand Canyon State
Bob and Dotty Martin

COLORADO'S HIGH THIRTEENERS
A Climbing and Hiking Guide
Mike Garratt and Bob Martin

HIGHPOINTS OF THE UNITED STATES
A Guide to the 50 State Summits
Don W. Holmes

MEXICO'S COPPER CANYON COUNTRY
A Hiking and Backpacking Guide
M. John Fayhee

ROCKY MOUNTAIN NATIONAL PARK DAYHIKER'S GUIDE
A Scenic Guide to 33 Favorite Hikes Including Longs Peak
Jerome Malitz

STATE PARKS OF THE MIDWEST: AMERICA'S HEARTLAND
A Guide to Camping, Fishing, Hiking, & Sightseeing
Vici DeHaan

STATE PARKS OF THE WEST
America's Best-Kept Secrets
A Guide to Camping, Fishing, Hiking, & Sightseeing
Vici DeHaan